COUNSELLING SKILLS

To Robert Kallaus

With very best wishes
Bob de Board.
Radmas 25/6/94

COUNSELLING SKILLS

Robert de Board

Gower

First published in hardback 1983 by
Gower Publishing Company Limited
Reprinted 1986

First paperback edition published 1987 by
Wildwood House Limited
Reprinted 1989
Reprinted 1994 by
Gower Publishing,
Gower House,
Croft Road,
Aldershot,
Hampshire GU11 3HR,
England.

ISBN 0 7045 0563 0

Typeset by Inforum Ltd, Portsmouth
Printed and bound in Great Britain by
Hartnolls Ltd, Bodmin, Cornwall.

'The degree to which I can create relationships which facilitate the growth of others as separate persons is a measure of the growth I have achieved myself. In some respects this is a disturbing thought, but it is also a promising or challenging one. It would indicate that if I am interested in creating helping relationships I have a fascinating lifetime job ahead of me, stretching and developing my potentialities in the direction of growth.'

Carl Rogers, *On Becoming a Person*

———

'Only connect'

E. M. Forster, *Howards End*

Contents

Preface

This book is written primarily for managers who would like to be able to give effective help to people at work, especially their subordinates. Work can provide intense feelings of satisfaction and achievement, but it can also cause a number of problems which make people feel sad and miserable; and, for some, it can create anxiety and stress.

Most people find ways of coping with their bad times and this usually involves talking to someone, often their marriage partner, a close friend or a sympathetic doctor or clergyman. But I believe that people who have problems at work should be able to find help at work, and especially from their manager.

It is very difficult to give a precise definition of a manager and what he does, and this difficulty reflects the subtle changes which have taken place in his role over the years. One of these changes involves the shift in the relationship between a manager and his subordinates. Attitudes to authority have changed significantly in the last twenty years and no doubt will continue to change. However, the manager still has the responsibility to get work done through his staff and he is still ultimately accountable for their performance. One of the great problems facing all organisations today is how a manager can exercise his legitimate and necessary authority in a style which is congruent with these changing attitudes.

It is my belief that the ability to counsel and to establish a counselling relationship is now a necessary addition to the managerial role and creates a management style which is appropriate to the spirit of the age. The present-day concept of counselling is a recent development and, in fact, is ahead of the dictionaries, which usually define counselling in terms of giving advice. According to the British Association of Counselling, 'the task of counselling is to give the client an opportunity to explore, discover and clarify ways of living more resourcefully and toward greater well-being'.

How far managers can add counselling to their role remains to be seen. In many company appraisal schemes, the interview is called an 'appraisal and counselling' interview but few managers receive any relevant guidance. Of course some managers do give effective and appropriate help to their staff and no doubt there are many people who counsel their boss! But, in my experience, these are exceptions rather than the rule.

In this book I have tried to explain what counselling means in practice and I have given some theories and ideas which help explain the process. I have tried to show the advantages of counselling and some of the pitfalls. My chief credential for writing this book is experience. Over the last ten years I have spent part of my non-working life as a counsellor and I currently spend time working with a medical practice with referred clients. As a member of the academic staff at Henley, The Management College, I am involved in training managers in counselling skills and

these occasions are frequently the high spots on the programme. Not, I must add, because of what I do, but because
the managers find counselling interesting and
stimulating and often exciting. It can also be puzzling and
frustrating, but it is never dull, and the process of learning
about it is never finished.

A note about terminology

When a manager agrees to his subordinate's request for
help, an unwritten contract is formed. It therefore seems
appropriate, in the context of the counselling relationship
discussed in this book, to refer to the manager as 'counsellor' and to the subordinate as 'client'. These descriptions
do not, of course, imply that any financial transaction is
involved.

A manager may be approached by a variety of people for
help at work and he will respond in the ways he thinks
best. But this book will explore those situations where a
manager is asked for help by his subordinate who, in that
relationship, becomes his client.

Robert de Board

1

Styles of Helping

How do you react when someone asks you for help? As a manager you may receive requests for help in a variety of ways. Someone may pop their head round the door and say 'Can you spare me a minute?' or 'Are you busy?' A subordinate may ask to make a formal appointment and you will book him or her in your diary for some time later that day. Sometimes requests for help come about in less obvious ways. You may be talking to someone and their agitated or sad appearance may appear to be an unspoken appeal for help, to which you could respond by saying 'You look upset. Can I help?' Or it may be that in an appraisal interview some aspect of your subordinate's performance is concerning you and you ask him if there is a problem about which he would like to talk to you.

Of course, every manager has the option *NOT* to give

help. You may be so busy that you don't want to be interrupted. You may feel a lack of sympathy with the person asking for help and feel that it is his job to solve his own problems without getting you involved. Or you may be perfectly aware that your subordinate is agitated and upset, but you don't want to get involved in his personal problems and so you give him no encouragement or opportunity to speak about them.

But let us suppose that you want to respond positively to a request for help. What are your options? There are two important factors which will affect the kind of help you give.

1. Your concern for the client or your concern for the problem

Suppose you are a technical expert and a subordinate comes to you with a tricky problem about which you have expert knowledge. You will be very interested and concerned with the problem and you will want to get all the facts in order to solve it. Your client (the subordinate) then becomes of less importance to you than the problem. If, for instance, I take my TV set to be repaired, I shall want the electrician to concentrate on the fault and not be very interested in me. In fact, I shall feel it inappropriate if he starts asking me how I am feeling and tries to establish an intimate relationship. In these instances, the helper is problem-centred rather than client-centred.

On the other hand, if I am not feeling well and visit my doctor for his help, I shall expect him to be concerned about me as a person and not just interested in my symptoms. If he is a good doctor, he will be more client-centred than problem-centred. But, if he is only concerned with my symptoms and, like a technical expert, simply gives me the pills and sends me packing, I shall not feel I have got the kind of help I was looking for.

A manager who is asked for help can thus be problem-centred or client-centred, and, as we shall see, these two approaches result in different kinds of help being given.

2. Including or excluding the client in solving the problem

Once a problem has been presented to the manager for help he has the option to collaborate and involve the client or to exclude the client and work at the problem on his own. If, for instance, you have a tax problem and seek help from an accountant, he will ask for all the facts and then probably say 'Right, leave it with me and I'll write to you in a week'. You may be very happy with this approach and feel that it is money well spent to have the problem solved for you. A manager may take exactly the same approach to a subordinate's problem and even when the subordinate remains in the room, the manager can act entirely on his own and simply give the subordinate an answer, based on his own experience, attitudes and knowledge. On the other hand, the manager can collaborate and work with his subordinate so that the subordinate is included in the problem-solving process and has to use his own brains as they work together.

A manager who is asked for help can elect to take the problem over and solve it himself or he can decide to include the client in the problem-solving process. Each approach will result in a different kind of help being given.

To re-state the situation so far: when a manager is asked for help, he can respond in a variety of ways. His responses will depend mainly on two factors:

1. Where he will show his greatest concern. He can
      (a) be more concerned with the client, or
      (b) be more concerned with the problem.
2. How he will work with the client. He can
      (a) include the client in solving the problem, or
      (b) exclude the client from solving the problem.

When these factors are put together, it shows that the manager can adopt one of four basic styles of helping.

THE BASIC STYLES OF HELPING

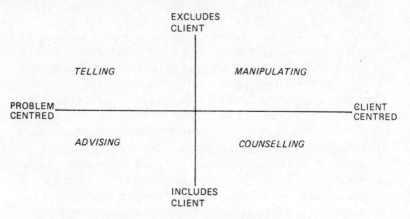

The four basic styles of helping are:

1. Telling   3. Manipulating
2. Advising   4. Counselling

Let us now look at each of them in more detail.

1. Telling

When the helper adopts the telling style he is more concerned with the problem than with the client and excludes
the client from the problem-solving process. As we have
already seen, this is the style most usually adopted by
technical experts who are asked for help with technical
problems. The helper takes over the problem and, having
got as much information as possible, uses his expertise to
solve it. Once he has got all the facts, he can virtually
ignore his client, whom he then sees as a person awaiting
an answer. People who typically adopt this style are
lawyers, tax consultants, medical consultants and virtually any technical specialist, who all end up by telling
their clients what to do. This is sometimes called the
'medical' model on the analogy of what happens when you
go to a doctor for help, for example, with a broken arm. The
doctor takes the problem over and you as a patient are

only passively involved in the healing process. The arm is set and put in plaster and your problem returned to you solved. As the client you have learnt very little about the way the problem was solved and if you were ever to break an arm again, you would have to go through the same process and seek exactly the same kind of help.

People who adopt the telling approach to helping must have expert knowledge (or believe they have) and must be able fully to understand the problem presented to them. They must be able to come up with the correct solution and be prepared to take responsibility for the outcome. They must believe that they know what is best for the client. They will limit the client's involvement to the minimum, usually requiring him or her merely to provide information. On the whole, the helper who tells his client what to do wants to maintain him in a dependent position. He hopes that if problems occur in the future he will be asked for help again. The teller is not concerned with the client's learning or development and in some cases will deliberately keep the client in ignorance of the methods he uses. The teller is likely to use such words as: 'What you must do is . . .' or 'Follow these instructions.' or 'Don't argue. Do it this way.' or 'If things start to go wrong, call me immediately.' or 'When you have another problem, I want you to send for me.'

2. Advising

When the helper adopts the advising style, he is more concerned with the problem than the client, but wants to include him in the problem-solving process. The adviser will want to get all the facts and details about the problem and then, using his skills and experience, will usually come up with a number of options and alternatives. He will present these to the client, explain their strengths and weaknesses and then get his client to select the one he thinks most appropriate. This approach is typically used by business consultants who want their clients to be involved in the problem-solving process so that they will be committed to the solution and responsible for its implementation. This style of helping is sometimes called the 'teaching' model, for the client will learn something from this approach and it is the way in which many teachers work with their pupils, helping them to recognise and select the right answer from a limited number of options.

People who adopt the advising style of helping, whilst they want their client to be involved, still want to retain the role of specialist. They need their specialist knowledge and skills to help them come up with possible solutions and they are usually capable and willing to be involved in implementing the solution, once this is chosen and agreed with the client. However, the adviser is always pulled in two ways as he tries to give honest and objective help. The first pressure on him is to give solutions which he personally is capable of implementing. Business consultants and specialists within an organisation are likely to suggest solutions which will suit their own particular strengths and interests. For instance, a computer specialist is likely to suggest answers to a business problem which will involve computer systems, even though there may be a much simpler solution. Similarly, if you visit a doctor with a stomach upset he is likely to diagnose the problem in physical terms and offer help accordingly. However, a psychiatrist might see the same problem in terms of stress and anxiety and psychological symptoms and suggest a different kind of help.

The other pressure on the adviser is to make proposals which are likely to please his client and not offend him. For example, a business consultant involved in helping a manager to reorganise his business might suggest restructuring the company in a way which is beneficial to the client himself, giving him a higher position or a bigger empire; in fact, the client may well be part of the original business problem, but the consultant may think it politic not to say so.

The helper who adopts the advising style is likely to use such phrases as: 'It seems to me there are several things you could do.' or 'Why don't you . . .' or 'Which of my ideas appeal to you?' or 'These are the options open to you.' or 'My advice to you is . . .' or 'I'm sure you've chosen the right answer.' or 'I was hoping you'd say that. It's what I thought all along.'

3. Manipulating

When a helper adopts a manipulating style, he is apparently more concerned with the client than the problem but he excludes the client from the problem-solving process. This is essentially an unfair use of influence and usually means that the helper thinks he knows what is best for the client. This approach is often used by members of the worst sort of religious sect who believe that if only people would join them and adopt their beliefs, all their problems would be solved. In such cases, it is often the person who is apparently the helper who needs help the most. Under the guise of helping, he manipulates his client in order to satisfy his own needs and desires. People who use this style often have the erroneous belief that they are born 'helpers' and therefore seek out people whom they believe are in some kind of trouble. The manipulator needs to keep his client in this dependent role and by a variety of subtle means, makes his client think that he really needs him. Both helper and client play a game which can only have one result – the client becomes more and more dependent on his 'helper' and vice-versa, whilst the real problem remains unsolved.

Of course, all helpers need clients to carry out their legitimate work. A doctor needs his patients and a business consultant needs his executive clients. But the helper should always be working toward the time when he won't be needed. The proof of effective help is when the client can stand on his own two feet.

The manipulator often has a low opinion of his client and wants to change him, either to the image of himself, or to the kind of person he would like to have been. Manipulative helpers can be very dangerous and should be avoided like the plague. They can often be recognised by the fact that they offer help before anyone has asked for it. They are essentially salesmen who have a product to sell and are continually looking for potential customers to buy their wares. However, real help rarely comes in packages and 'off-the-shelf' advice has little value. Such people are likely to say 'Won't you let me help you?' or 'I've noticed you're in trouble. I know just the thing for you.' or 'Why don't we have a little talk?' or 'If I were you . . .'

4. Counselling

The helper who adopts a counselling style is more concerned with the client than with the problem and involves the client in solving the problem. There are very significant differences between this style and the other three.

The first is that the counsellor need not have detailed specialist knowledge about the problem presented to him for help. Common sense suggests that he should have enough awareness and knowledge to be able to ask intelligent and appropriate questions. But in the last analysis his success in providing help depends more on his knowledge of human nature and his empathy with his client, than on a detailed knowledge of the problem being discussed.

Secondly, he does not need to formulate a solution. When he begins to counsel somebody he may have no idea of the outcome and, indeed, may feel rather helpless himself.

The third important difference is that the aim of the counsellor is to enable his client to find his own solution to his problem. The helper who counsels does not take over the problem in any way from his client. In fact, he helps him to take full responsibility for it and is happy to withdraw as soon as possible. The counsellor never offers advice and never criticises his client. He believes that the client knows what is best for himself and helps him to discover what this is. The counsellor listens rather than talks, and uses his questioning skills to help his client explore and analyse the problem in all its aspects.

Another difference between counselling and other forms of helping is that the counsellor wants the client to learn as much as possible through the problem-solving process, so that when he has another problem, he is much better equipped to deal with it himself. Because he is client-centred rather than problem-centred, he values his client as a person and is genuinely interested in his feelings and emotions and recognises that these are just as much connected with the problem as the more objective facts.

The counsellor is likely to use such phrases as: 'What seems to be the problem?' or 'Why is it worrying you?' or 'What do you think?' or 'How did that make you feel?' or 'Do you want to talk about it?' or 'If you do that, what do you think will happen?'

WHY USE COUNSELLING?

After reading this, many managers will recognise themselves as tellers and advisers. These are legitimate and effective ways of helping subordinates, and others, although it is clear that an effective helping style depends very much on the nature of the problem. Telling is a good response to a direct request for technical help. It is quick and results in the problem being solved and progress being made. In response to a request for advice, it may be appropriate to act as adviser and put forward good and viable solutions which the client may never have thought of himself, and allow him to select a course of action which now seems right to him. But what are the advantages of counselling? These are set out below.

1. Counselling is an effective way to help someone with their personal problems. Technical problems at work rarely worry people for long. There is usually an expert or a specialist on hand who – given the time and resources –

can come up with the right answer and tell or advise them what to do.

But personal problems are different and require a different kind of help. For instance, a man approaching the age of 50 who realises that he will not get further promotion may find the thought of another ten years in the same job very depressing. As well as this, he may compare his career progress with that of his contemporaries and feel that he has done badly. This is a real problem which will affect his performance and he may approach his boss for help. What helping style should the boss adopt? Telling? 'Look here, Brian, you've got to get a grip on yourself, and stop having these morbid thoughts. Get stuck into the job and before you know it, it will be retirement time.' Or advising? 'Brian, it seems to me you've got three options. You could take early retirement at 55, which is only another five years. Or you could hand in your notice now, although I suppose you've still got the mortgage to pay. Or, of course, you can always soldier on and hope things improve. What do you think?'

A manager could take either of these approaches but it is unlikely that they would provide any lasting help for the depressed Brian. What he is looking for is someone who, for a start, will listen to him and let him spill out his fears and sadness, even though some of it may sound silly, even to himself. He wants someone to show a real interest in him so that he has the courage and strength really to examine his situation and recognise all the implications. And then he wants help to explore the opportunities open to him so that he can make up his own mind about what he should do.

In other words, he is looking for a counsellor. The problem is whether he can find one or not. He may be able to get this kind of help from a clergyman or an understanding GP. Perhaps he has a wife who can give him wise counsel. But the concern of this book is that he should get this kind of help from his boss.

The above example is only one of the hundreds of personal problems which affect people at work. Each unresolved problem of this kind not only adds to the sum of human unhappiness, but also reduces people's efficiency.

Counselling is a way of helping people deal with their personal problems in a way which telling or advising can never achieve.

2. Counselling results in decisions that 'stick'. When people are offered help, there are essentially four ways in which they can react.

(a) They can reject help.

(b) They can accept the help and advice because they are coerced into accepting it. If they don't accept, they fear they may incur the displeasure of the helper who may operate some sort of sanction against them. Some managers who are tellers and advisers can get very upset and even angry if their solutions are not accepted, even when they are offering help with sensitive personal matters. So their subordinates accept their proposals because they feel forced to do so.

(c) They accept the help offered because they like and respect the helper and in some way identify with him. Some helpers are very charismatic and seem to exude an air of mystical wisdom. However, there are very few charismatic managers, and trying to be liked by everyone is an exhausting business. And when it happens, as it must, that the charismatic helper is discovered to have feet of clay, he loses all credibility.

(d) They accept the help offered because they themselves have been enabled to work through the problem and are pesonally involved in the final decision and solution. They have gone through the process of internalising, that is, taking the ideas inside themselves and making them their own. When this happens, the individual is committed to implementing the solution, not because anyone has forced him to do so, but because he has made a personal decision. This process of internalising results from counselling: the client says 'I did it myself', and he is determined to carry out the solution he himself has reached.

3. Counselling results in human growth and development. People who, when they seek help, are always told or advised what to do, can never grow. All they learn is whom to ask for help. But counselling, because it forces the client to think for himself, can provide him with opportunities for growth and, more importantly, with opportunities for change. Some adults have difficulty abandoning the patterns of behaviour established in childhood: they may look for helpers who will behave like parents and treat them like children, giving them either love and praise or criticism and punishment.

Counselling can break this pattern and enable people to think for themselves and make decisions that are right for them. Counselling helps them to face the reality of their own autonomy and enables them to realise that they are free to choose. The counsellor is not a father-figure, but simply an adult working with another adult who has neither to be pleased nor feared. Managers who can achieve this kind of relationship with their subordinates and provide help through counselling, enable them to grow and develop in ways which no training course can ever achieve.

4. Counselling is in tune with changing attitudes towards authority. There is no doubt that society in Britain and in many other countries has undergone profound changes in the last 30 years. The old authority figures, such as clergymen, doctors and the aristocracy, no longer demand or obtain automatic respect. Political leaders are more likely to be criticised than praised. There is a much greater demand for participation and involvement in decision-making at all levels of society. People increasingly challenge authority: 'Why should I? Who does he think he is?' These attitudes are encouraged by the educational system which says 'Think for yourself. Make up your own mind.'

However, in spite of the increasing challenge to authority, people still need leaders and leadership as much as they ever did. In spite of widespread cynicism and disillusion with politics, the selection and appointment of leaders, such as a prime mininster or president, send a country into a paroxysm of anxiety, while the death of a Pope and the selection of his successor are of immense international concern. At the parochial level, the appointment of leaders in any kind of organisation, from the gardening club to the village preservation society, still creates intense activity and can turn gentle citizens into furious campaigners.

When one leader goes and a new one has yet to be appointed, people really do feel leaderless; whether it concerns their church or their country it worries and frightens them. Groups and societies need leaders if only to criticise and attack, and the lack of one arouses the emotions and creates intense anxiety. One of the problems facing leaders today is how to find a leadership style that is appropriate to these changing social attitudes and yet allows them to exercise their legitimate authority.

The manager faces exactly the same dilemma. His work team is likely to have these anti-authoritarian attitudes and will expect to be increasingly consulted and involved with what is going on. They want to challenge established systems and procedures and to examine any new proposals and changes. They do not want passively to accept orders and are unlikely to give automatic respect to their manager.

And yet they want leadership. They need a manager who is visibly seen to be in charge and who they know carries the ultimate responsibility for their group. They want a manager who has evolved a leadership style which recognises and adapts to their attitudes and who, at the same time, is effective and gets the job done.

The image of the old-style 'hire-and-fire' boss, the bullying autocrat, is as abhorent to most managers as it is to the workforce. The struggle for many managers today is how to find a style which takes into account current attitudes and yet enables them to exercise their proper and necessary authority.

Counselling is one way of doing this. It allows the manager to show a real concern for the people working for him. It enables him to facilitate their growth and development. It allows him to recognise and communicate the bounds of his authority and to make his subordinates realise the real and inevitable consequences of crossing them. It provides his subordinates with opportunities to analyse and clarify problems and create and test new ideas and ways or working.

SUMMARY

When a manager is asked for help by a subordinate his response will depend on two factors.

(a) His concern for the subordinate himself or the problem he brings. Will he be client-centred or problem-centred?

(b) The way in which he works on the problem, either on his own or with the client. Will he include or exclude him in the problem-solving process?

When these factors are combined it can be seen that there are four basic helping styles which anyone can adopt and each will have a different effect: telling, advising, manipulating and counselling.

1. Telling

The person who gives help by telling his client what to do, is problem-centred and excludes the client from the problem-solving process. This style is frequently adopted by technical experts whose skill and knowledge enable them to give the right answer.

2. Advising

The person who helps by giving advice is problem-centred and includes his client in problem-solving. The adviser frequently develops options and then gets the client to select the one he favours. The danger is that he will offer solutions which require his own expertise and which will not offend his client.

3. Manipulating

The person who uses a manipulating style is apparently client-centred but in fact excludes the client from the

problem-solving process. Such a person uses his client to
satisfy his own needs and wants to keep him in a highly-
dependent role. Manipulative helpers can often be recognised by the fact that they offer help before anyone has
requested it.

4. Counselling

Counselling is a style of helping which is client-centred
and involves the client in solving the problem. It is significantly different from the other three styles and aims to
help the client find solutions to his own problems.

WHY USE COUNSELLING?

Telling and advising people how to solve their problems
can be effective ways for managers to give help, especially
when the problems are technical ones. But counselling has
specific advantages over the other helping styles.

1. It provides effective help with personal problems.
When a subordinate has a personal problem he is looking for someone who can help him explore what is
troubling him and eventually help him make up his own
mind what he should do. Unresolved problems not only
cause unhappiness but also reduce efficiency, and counselling is an effective way to deal with this.

2. It results in decisions that 'stick'. A person at work
will only be committed to making a change in his attitude or behaviour if he has personally thought the
problem through and reached his own decision. Good
counselling enables this process of internalisation to
take place, resulting in the subordinate being determined to carry out the changes he himself has decided
upon.

3. It results in growth and development. Counselling
helps and encourages people to think for themselves.

Through being involved in the problem-solving process, the client learns more about himself, develops his own resources and abilities, and becomes better equipped to manage future problems.

4. It is in tune with current social attitudes. In an age when authority is questioned and where the education system encourages a 'make-up-your-own-mind' attitude, there is still a real need for leadership. Counselling is one way in which a manager can exercise his authority effectively but in a non-authoritarian manner.

2

Predicting People's Problems

All managers have to solve problems. Their professional training and experience are geared to improving their problem-solving ability. When promotion comes it always involves an increased responsibility for solving bigger and better problems. A problem in managerial terms is any situation where reality differs from expectations in an adverse way. For instance, there is a problem in cash flow when revenue is less than the planned amount. There is a production problem when output is less than predicted and there is a problem with supplies when what is available is less than required.

It might be expected that as managerial skills in problem-solving increase and are added to the total experience of organisations, fewer problems would occur, or that those which do occur would be solved more easily.

It might seem, in other words, that as the body of managerial knowledge grows, the reality of business life should become closer to management's plans and forecasts. Paradoxically, this does not appear to be the case. Many managers would argue that, in fact, their problems are increasing in number and complexity. The micro-chip may well herald a new industrial revolution but it will also bring many managerial headaches. The electronic office will need an old-fashioned medicine cabinet for the aspirin. Fritz Schumacher, author of *Small is Beautiful*, pointed out this same paradox with regard to science in his last book, *Good Work*, (p.98):

> Another illusion which is still rampant is that science can solve all problems. I have no doubt that science can solve any individual problem when it is clearly defined. But my experience is that as it solves problem 'A', it creates a whole host of new problems. It's quite a thought that there are more scientists alive today than there have been in all previous human history taken together. What do they all do? They solve problems very efficiently. Aren't we running out of problems? No. We have more and more. This seems to be a bottomless pit. They grow faster than we solve them. So this is where we have to ask 'What on earth is going on here?'

So, what on earth is going on in organisations, when there are more and more managers who have never been so well educated and trained and yet the problems facing them are increasing both in number and complexity?

One way to answer this question is to look at the kinds of problems facing managers and these, I suggest, fall into two main categories, (a) technical and, (b) human. These are the twin aspects of every manager's job and yet it is remarkable that the human one still comes a very poor second in the real world of business. Although there is an explosion of books on psychology and courses about behavioural science, the technical aspect of work is still seen to be the main managerial task in most factories and offices. Promotions to executive posts are usually made on the criterion of technical ability. A senior director was once heard to say 'I don't give a damn if he's good with people or not. Can he get those car bodies moving off the production line?'

This idea is particularly prevalent in the professions. Scientists, engineers and accountants, for instance, undertake long and exhaustive technical training, and consequently tend to judge people's performance solely in terms of technical skill. Yet it is common experience that as a person moves up through an organisation, he is involved less and less in technical work and more with the human problems of leadership, co-operation and the co-ordination of other people's work.

Can 'people-problems' be predicted in organisations or must managers continue to be surprised and perplexed by the problems that seem continually to face them? Undoubtedly the basic predictors are those learnt through experience: an intelligent manager learns to recognise the pattern of events and situations which usually result in problems and so takes avoiding action. But experience takes time to acquire and is, by definition, not available to the young or newly appointed manager; furthermore, not everyone has the inclination or ability to learn from their experience.

As well as experience, however, there are a number of ideas and theories which are helpful in trying to predict when and where people-problems may occur. Elliott Jacques has proposed the idea that people at work will be problem free (he calls this a state of 'psychological equilibrium') when the work they do is just matched by their capacity to do it and for that work they receive payment which is felt to be equitable. Thus, there are clearly three areas which can cause problems:

(a) When people feel their pay is unequitable for the work they do and the responsibilities they carry. It should be noted that this includes feeling overpaid as well as the more obvious feeling of underpayment.

(b) The nature and content of the work itself. Is it too easy or too demanding?

(c) The capacity of the individual to carry out the work he is given to do.

Using these three concepts, Jacques is able to describe 12 possible situations which can cause a person at work to feel dissatisfaction and therefore to have a personal problem ('Equitable Payment' Chapter 12).

Another fruitful source of ideas which can help managers predict people-problems is in the writing of Freud. In *Group Psychology and the Analysis of the Ego* (Chapter 1) he attempts to analyse the processes which occur when a group or an organisation form. He says that there are two important factors in this process:

(a) Leadership – the group coalesces around a leader and therefore the group cannot form until his authority is established and accepted.

(b) Interpersonal relations – once everyone accepts the leader, they then have a common focus and can form relationships with each other.

I have personally found this idea to have the greatest practical value when working with groups or consulting with organisations. I believe I can now predict that when there are serious problems preventing a group from working, it will involve either the authority of the leader ('Who does he think he is?' 'How did he get appointed?'), or bad relations between the members ('How do they think I could work with so and so?' 'I can't stand his attitude').

There are, of course, many other theories and ideas which can help in prediction, especially those concerning motivation and satisfaction. For instance, Herzberg's famous 'Motivation – Hygiene' theory can provide a checklist of factors which may cause a person to have a problem, such as poor supervision, bad working conditions, lack of responsibility, and so on.

CATEGORISING PEOPLE-PROBLEMS

If a person at work has a problem, what is likely to be causing it? Excluding those problems which can be solved by the application of technical skills, i.e. plant breakdown,

computer malfunction, etc., people-problems can be grouped into (at least) three categories:
- Personality problems
- Organisational problems
- External problems.

1. Personality problems

Some people have problems or can cause them, simply by the way they are and the way they behave. They may be worried and depressed by lack of confidence or feelings of unworthiness, or else they may be arrogant and dominating, continually causing rows and upsets. The problems caused by these kinds of behaviour arise not from the organisation, but from the individual. He carries this way of behaving around with him, no matter where he works or what he does. In many ways, these problems are the most difficult to solve and cause the greatest difficulties at work. Table 1 outlines types of behaviour which may indicate that the problem is of this nature.

2. Organisational problems

Many people-problems are the direct result of human beings living and working together in the same organisation. Anyone can tell if they have an organisational problem by simply asking the question 'Would I still have this problem if I left this organisation?' If the answer is 'no', then it is an organisational problem.

Problems of this kind can be fairly well predicted on the basis of past experience, together with some of the theories and ideas mentioned previously. They are likely to be caused by issues of authority, poor interpersonal relations, payment not felt to be equitable, overwork, boredom, lack of promotion and so on.

Because these problems are a function of the organisation, they should all be capable of being resolved within it. Regretfully this is rarely so. Many organisations have grown so quickly and have been so engrossed with their progress, or else have been so badly managed, that they have failed to develop this self-correcting mechanism. All too often an organisation is judged to be healthy and dynamic on such crude criteria as profits or technological advancement. I believe that for success in the future, all organisations will have to devise ways in which organisational people-problems can be solved – or at least helped – within the organisation. Those that don't will suffer the same fate as the dinosaurs, doomed to extinction because they failed to adapt to the changing environment.

There is some hard evidence concerning the problems which people have at work. In the early 1920s the Western Electric Company in Chicago initiated a unique programme of research into the effect of work on human performance. This was supervised by Professor Elton Mayo and his colleagues from Harvard and is known generally as the 'Hawthorne Experiments' (Dickson and Roethlisberger, 1966).

One part of this work was a long-term programme of counselling which lasted from 1936 to 1955. The counsellors were full-time independent professionals and were not part of management. The programme started with five counsellors and this number steadily increased until 1948 when there were 55 counsellors covering a workforce of 21,000. From then on, the number of counsellors began to fall and when the programme ended in 1955 there were only eight.

The terms of reference were very wide. Any employee could request an interview with his counsellor, and the counsellor could request an interview with an employee. Confidentiality was maintained and complete records were kept of all the interviews. For what reasons did employees visit the counsellors? When the reports were analysed, they revealed that the counselling sessions dealt mainly with the following five concerns of employees:

1 Keeping and losing a job
2 Unsatisfactory work relations

Problem	Minor	Serious	Acute/Chronic
POOR SELF–IMAGE AND A HIGH OPINION OF OTHERS	Humble, timid, anxious to please, unsure of himself, uncertain of the future. Wants to 'help' rather than to 'do'. Tells anecdotes of his past mistakes and blunders. Easily influenced. Always searching for a 'real' friend.	Cannot accept success or achievement. Worries over possible failure. Seeks excuses for avoiding responsibility. Indecisive. Dependent. Wants a 'special' relationship rather than group membership.	Opts out of decision - making Withdraws from personal relationships. Cynical about making improvements. Envious of others' achievements. Suffers from depression.
OVER–ESTIMATION OF OWN ABILITY	Talks at you. Very definite views. Aggressive. Ready to take people on. Looks out for fools so as not to suffer them gladly. Dominates meetings. Has a temper. Boring.	Autocratic, not open to influence, fixed views on all issues. Critical of colleagues and subordinates. Boastful. Makes quick decisions. Dislikes participation. Won't delegate. Gets angry. Wants to control others.	Bullying, arrogant. Ignores facts, plays hunches. Contemptuous of other people. Enjoys triumphing over others. Won't tolerate criticism. High blood pressure.
POOR SELF–IMAGE AND LOW OPINION OF OTHERS	Self-pitying, anxious, muddled. Poor work organisation. Blames others for own mistakes. Worried that 'they' may be watching him. Few friends.	Confused and inconsistent. Increasing load of unfinished work. Forgetful. Fairly sure that 'they' are getting at him. Defensive, lonely. Secretive.	Irrational. Work organisation chaotic. Jobs never completed. Isolated. Paranoid. Heading for 'breakdown'

Table 1.   Personality problems – behaviour predictors

3   Felt injustices
4   Unsatisfactory relations with authority
5   Job development.

(You will recall that Freud's theory of group behaviour showed that interpersonal relationships and authority issues were likely to be significant major factors. Items 2 and 4 give empirical evidence for this.)

However, it is my experience that the principal causes of anxiety within organisations can be classified as follows:

– Technical incompetence
– Underwork (role underload)
– Overwork (role overload)
– Uncertain future
– Relationships.

Every individual will reveal his anxiety in his own way, but it is to some extent possible to generalise, and Table 2 sets out some of the behaviour characteristics one might expect to observe in people with problems of this kind.

3. External problems

For every employee in an organisation, at whatever level, work is only one part of life. The three major parts of life are work, family and leisure: but they are each part of the same life lived by the same person. Each of these parts of life have a profound effect on the total person and his behaviour, wherever he is and whatever he is doing. When a person is at work, he inevitably brings with him the emotions and feelings generated from outside and of course when he leaves the office or factory, he takes with him the effect of these work experiences. This continual interplay and interchange goes some way to explaining the varied and sometimes extraordinary problems which people will confide to their manager.

How far a manager should go in dealing with problems of a personal or even intimate nature will depend on the individual manager and the relationship he has with the

	Minor	Serious	Acute/Chronic
TECHNICAL INCOMPETENCE	Unsure of some work or office procedures or technical processes and systems.	Unable to grasp all details of processes and systems for which he is accountable. Has made, or at least fears he will make, a serious error.	Cannot assimilate new ideas and technology. Unable, or unwilling to make decisions. Bad relations with technical experts and new graduates. Frequently absent with bilious attacks.
UNDERWORK	Occasionally bored by lack of work or work that is undemanding.	Feels continually bored and talents underemployed. Concerned by lack of demanding work. Always reads 'job vacancies' in the paper. Begins to have poor timekeeping record.	Casual or cynical attitude to work. Nothing seems important Increased pre-lunch drinking. Weekend starts on Thursday. Projects never get completed. Increased flirtation.
OVERWORK	Sometimes overwhelmed by pressure of work, sudden panics and crises.	Continually attending meetings, always on the phone, takes work home. Too much travelling. Everything is urgent and needed yesterday. Social life contracting. Always tired.	Continually agitated. Loss of contact with staff. Works longer hours but backlog of work increasing. Sleeps badly and has increasing rows at home. Social life vanishing. Starts to take Valium.
UNCERTAIN FUTURE	Concerned about next promotion move. When and where to?	Worried by lack of promotion. Younger people moving past him. Has he reached his ceiling? Soothing noises from boss, but no definite statement of career plans.	Frightened by lack of promotion. Undertakes more and more work to prove his ability. Envious of colleagues' status and possessions. Increasing bank overdraft to 'keep up with the Jones's'
RELATIONSHIPS	Concerned by lack of friends at work and the feeling of not belonging.	Feels isolated and ignored. Attempts at friendship seem to fail. Has a poor self-image and worries about lack of qualifications. Increased paranoia. Are they 'getting at him?'	Increasingly withdrawn. Eats lunch on his own. Sarcastic and cynical about the organisation. His department appears increasingly chaotic. At meetings negative and uncooperative. Avoids personal contacts—uses memos.

Table 2. Organisational problems – behaviour predictors

subordinate. Every manager learns to recognise the problems he can cope with and those which he should refer to
another, possibly more professional, agency. However, the
effective counsellor learns never to be surprised at the
oddness of human behaviour or the intricate and
seemingly stupid situations into which people can get
themselves.

Marriage By far the largest number of problems arising
outside work are related to marriage. Every counsellor
needs to recognise that couples live 'happily ever after'
only in stories, and that any marriage is likely to have as
many bad times as good. He will also know that there are
always two sides to these problems and that he is only
hearing one of them. He realises that by 'taking sides' he
would be compounding the problem; his job is rather to
help the person explore and understand the total situation. This friendly but essentially neutral approach is
difficult to maintain, especially if the manager knows the
family concerned and is friendly with them. But from my
own experience, this is the most helpful approach. The
worst approach of all is for the manager, albeit with the
best of motives, to agree with all the person says, thus
colluding with him. This may well contribute to a deterio-
ration in the situation.

Bereavement The death of a close friend or relative, and
especially the death of a partner, is one of the hardest
blows anyone can suffer. Death has replaced sex as
society's 'tabu' subject and many people are embarrassed
when they meet someone who has recently been bereaved.
They usually give what appears to be good advice and
encourage the person to keep working and to make sure
they are always busy. But in fact what every bereaved
person needs to do is to mourn the loss of their loved one.
Less sophisticated societies than ours know the truth of
this and have ceremonies and rituals which allow for and
encourage an open show of grief. There is a lot of evidence
to show that people who are unable to mourn, or are
discouraged from doing so, store up all kinds of psychological problems for the future.

Bereavement can bring about a variety of feelings which may include sadness, anger and guilt; these all take time to be expressed and worked through. It is interesting to note that Freud speaks of the 'work of mourning' to indicate that it requires a great deal of mental and emotional energy and effort.

Helpful counselling for a bereaved person allows him or her to talk about the person who has died and possibly the circumstances surrounding the death. Often the anger felt at a death is not simply due to the loss of a loved one, but anger at a world that doesn't notice and doesn't care.

Of course, death is a frightening and fearful thing and any death causes us, in some way, to be aware of our own mortality. As John Donne wrote, 'Never send to know for whom the bell tolls. It tolls for thee.' A counsellor who can offer a person the opportunity to talk about his bereavement, within a supportive and caring relationship, is providing the most valuable help.

This sort of counselling requires the ability to talk of death without getting upset oneself and also not to be anxious at the expression of grief. In one incident, a manager came rushing out of his office, looking very distraught, saying 'Come quick. Jack's broken down!' What had happened was that Jack was crying! An effective counsellor will not be frightened if the person breaks down and cries. Rather, he knows that this is good and that he is enabling that person to come to grips with his own sadness and gradually work through it.

Depression Depression is an 'umbrella' term used to cover a variety of painful emotional states. It may refer to a passing mood of 'being down in the dumps' or to a more or less permanent state of misery. There are clearly many situations which are sad and depressing and everyone experiences feelings of depression at some time. This is called 'reactive' depression and may result from a bereavement, the loss of a job, failure to get promotion, a marriage break-up, etc. Counselling someone who is suffering from this kind of depression requires great skill and sensitivity, and the manager may feel that he is not equipped to cope. However, it is hard to know who *is* equipped to cope! Not every doctor has the time or skill to listen, and the result is an enormous number of prescriptions for anti-depressant drugs – which can never solve the problem.

Counselling is difficult in these cases because when people are very depressed their whole view of themselves and of the world becomes negative and pessimistic. Everything is interpreted in terms of gloom and failure and even the most joyful events are experienced in terms of unhappiness. The counsellor must listen attentively and sympathetically, and, by asking sensitive questions, allow the person to explore his feelings. The more the person can be helped to explore the reality of his problem, the sooner will he start to come to terms with his feelings and begin to consider doing something about them. Under no circumstances will the counsellor tell the person to 'snap out of it': he realises that this is not possible.

There is a more serious form of depression called 'endogenous' depression, which is an illness, and appears not to be linked with any obvious event or cause. This form of illness affects probably one in fifteen of the population and clearly needs professional help.

The typical depression seen in older, obsessive people is characterised by continual tiredness, lack of drive, finding everything an effort and feeling worse in the mornings and better as the day wears on. Sleep is disturbed by early morning waking, often with a sense of dread. Appetite, weight and sexual drive are reduced. There is a lack of initiative, a tendency to worry about trivia, a gloomy outlook which disturbs judgement and loss of normal aggressiveness. There is a tendency to drink more alcohol and to smoke more heavily.
(*The BMA Book of Executive Health*)

The causes of this illness are still uncertain. It may be due to a chemical imbalance and it frequently does respond to drug therapy. It may also be due to unconscious psychological processes with unexpressed feelings which result in feelings of self-hatred. If the manager thinks that a subordinate is suffering from severe depression, he should urge that person to seek professional advice, which, in the first instance, means consulting his G.P.

Fortunately these illnesses have an excellent prognosis with treatment and once the individual has recovered there is no impairment of psychological integrity. It is worth repeating here that such illnesses are not necessarily a result of work difficulty, although to the sick patient work becomes an intolerable burden and may be blamed. There are many other precipitants, from unexpressed grief or anger, the effect of certain drugs including alcohol and after-effects of severe infections or surgical operations, to the effect of hormones, including in some women the contraceptive pill. It is important to consider such possibilities carefully before reducing the level of responsibility of someone who may have spent much of his life attaining a position that, with help, he is still capable of fulfilling. *(The BMA Book of Executive Health)*

SUMMARY

A. Solving problems is an integral part of every manager's job and each promotion brings responsibility for solving bigger and more complex ones. In spite of improved management education, problems at work seem to increase rather than decrease. This is because the problems which cause managers the greatest worry and concern usually involve human factors. There are some useful theories and ideas which can help managers predict possible problem situations.

1. Elliott Jaques suggests that three factors must be in balance if a person is to be in a state of 'psychological equilibrium'. These are:
    (a) An equitable payment (i.e. payment that is felt to be fair)
    (b) The content of the work itself
    (c) The capacity of the individual.
2. Freud argues that a group or organisation must resolve two important issues before it can work effectively. These are:
    (a) The authority and position of the leader
    (b) The interpersonal relationships between the members.
3. Herzberg's 'Motivation – Hygiene' theory indicates that dissatisfaction is likely to arise from the 'Hygiene Factors', which comprise company policy and administration, supervision, salary, interpersonal relations and working conditions.

B. People-problems fall into three categories: personality, organisational and external problems.

1. Personality problems stem from the nature of the individual himself and manifest themselves in the way he behaves, no matter where he is. These problems may arise because an individual has:
    (a) A poor self-image but a high opinion of others
    (b) An over-estimation of his own abilities

(c) A poor self-image and a low opinion of other people.

2. Organisational problems: these kinds of people-problems are the direct result of people living and working together in the same organisation. They should therefore be capable of being resolved within the organisation and counselling is one way of doing this.

In a 20-year counselling programme in the USA an analysis showed that employees visited their counsellors with five primary concerns:

(a) Keeping and losing a job
(b) Unsatisfactory work relations
(c) Felt injustices
(d) Unsatisfactory relations with authority
(e) Job development.

Another classification of organisational problems are:

(a) Technical incompetence
(b) Underwork (role underload)
(c) Overwork (role overload)
(d) Uncertain future
(e) Relationships.

3. External problems: problems that arise outside the organisation can obviously affect performance at work. How far a manager should be prepared to offer help on these personal and intimate problems depends on his relationship with the person in trouble and the confidence he has in his own counselling abilities. These problems can be many and various, but frequently include:

(a) Marriage
(b) Bereavement
(c) Depression.

REFERENCES

Dickson, J.D., and Roethisberger, F.J., *Counselling in an Organisation,* Harvard University, Boston, 1966

Jaques, E., *Equitable Payment,* Heinemann, 1961 (Especially Chapter 5 'Conditions for Psycho-Economic equilibrium')

Freud, S., *Group Psychology and the Analysis of the Ego,* Hogarth Press (Standard Edition of the complete works of Sigmund Freud), 1959

Schumacher, F., *Good Work,* Cape, 1979

3

The Elements of Counselling

The prime aim of counselling is to help the individual discover the solutions to his own problems. This may go against a natural inclination to give advice, especially in a boss-subordinate relationship. People only become committed to a particular decision or course of action when they have made up their own minds and personally believe that it is the right thing to do. This fact is at the centre of positive motivation. Whilst money, conditions, and the type of work are all contributory factors to the motivation of people at work, the essential factor is the personal commitment which a person brings to their work. When it becomes 'my work' and not 'his work', I start working for myself and use all my own internal energy and standards and enjoy all the potential psychological rewards. The effective counsellor acknowledges this process and attempts to work with it.

What is right for me is not necessarily right for someone else and what is important to me is not automatically important to others. The counsellor recognises an individual's autonomy and potential power, attempts to realise and release this power, rather than to deny or fight it. In a counselling interview between a manager and his subordinate, the manager recognises that his own power and authority are important factors. Equally important are the subordinate's own standards and aspirations and the potential energy they can release.

Counselling aims to help a person find his own solution to a problem. Set out below are some important aspects of effective counselling.

Listening

Listening need not be passive activity and Carl Rogers has coined the description 'active listening'. This means doing something positive rather than simply refraining from talking! It involves an attitude of mind and body which sends out the non-verbal message to the person being counselled: 'At this moment you are the most important person in my world. What you are saying interests and concerns me. You have my full attention.' Different people will do this in different ways but there will be certain things common to all. There will be plenty of eye contact. There will be no interruptions until the person has obviously finished speaking. The counsellor will be physically alert, indicating a genuine interest in what is being said.

Perhaps the biggest obstacle to active listening is the desire to think ahead and plan the next question. The counsellor communicates that this is happening by a variety of signals which together say 'I want to interrupt now'; he withdraws his attention from what the person is saying and gives it to the question he is forming.

Active listening has at least two positive benefits in counselling. The first and obvious one is that it provides information for further discussion and action. The second is that it undoubtedly has a therapeutic effect. Talking to an attentive listener enables people to externalise their problems, which is the first step to getting rid of them, and it can give great emotional release. Linked with this is the confirmation which an attentive listener automatically gives to a speaker, of their importance as a person.

The 'presenting' problem

It can be difficult to start a counselling interview. The way in which this happens depends on the relationship which already exists between the manager and his subordinate and also on the problems which both hope, or fear, will be discussed. However, from the subordinate's point of view, the more serious or delicate the issue he wishes to raise, the more difficulty he will find in broaching it. His first words are unlikely to be a full statement of the problem. He will find it easier to start by stating the problem in broad terms, in such a way that the boss is unlikely to react sharply. Consciously or unconsciously, he will be saying sufficient to enable him to go further, if the climate feels 'right', or if necessary, to withdraw without having given too much away. He may be struggling internally, seeing how much he can admit to himself and what defence mechanisms he can cease to operate.

The practical response required from the counsellor in this situation is to listen intently and be prepared to help the subordinate open up and go further towards the heart of the matter.

Finding the core problem

This follows naturally from understanding the difficulty of presenting the problem. Statements made by the subordinate at the start of a counselling interview, always contain clues, or linkages, to the essence of the problem – the thing which is concerning him personally at that very moment. Statements such as 'I'm worried about the paperwork at the office', or 'I'm concerned with the poor relationships in the department', are generalities which, if taken as the full statement of the problem would result in non-effective action. A good counsellor will understand the reason for the general statement and by appropriate questions, enable the person to speak of the core problem; this will always be something to do with his personal situation at the present time, and will usually involve some other person or persons.

Recognising and admitting feelings

Every problem brought for counselling is concerned with a person's feelings. Problems that are purely technical don't require counselling, but can be solved by factual answers. (However, it should be noted that a problem which is presented as a purely technical one may frequently have an emotional aspect as well.) The exploration and recognition of emotions can be extremely difficult for a manager. Part of a subordinate's problem may be the fear of not being up to the job, or the fear of redundancy. Or it could be that he feels anxious about his promotion prospects or salary level. Whatever the problem, an effective counsellor knows that it cannot be fully resolved unless or until the associated 'feelings' have been dealt with. The subordinate must be given not only the opportunity to express his feelings, which he may be in the habit of concealing, but also the help to explore and clarify what these are. This kind of counselling work requires sensitivity, but in my own experience it is the key to effectiveness, and results in problem resolution, personal growth and self-insight.

Criticism

The one thing guaranteed to stop effective counselling is criticism. When people are criticised, they feel threatened and the automatic psychological responses are fight or flight. The fight response is obvious enough and may take the form of 'What do you mean, my work's not up to scratch? You're never around to see it!' The flight response is usually a little more subtle but it involves moving on from the topic as quickly as possible. It might involve an apology – 'I'm very sorry, it won't happen again' – or else a string of excuses. Either way the person who feels criticised is putting into operation his defence mechanisms to protect himself from the perceived threat. The climate of openness and trust, essential for effective counselling, has changed and it takes a long time for it to be re-established. The interview may continue, but no further useful work will be done.

Some managers find this difficult to accept, believing that it may be appropriate to criticise a subordinate. Criticism may have its uses, but in the counselling relationship, it is simply counter-productive.

Problem-solving

Counselling is all about helping people to solve their own problems. But the situation is rarely clear cut – presumably if it were so, then there would be no problem. Whilst no formula can be given for a counselling interview, it is likely to contain the following elements (not necessarily in this order):

1. The presenting problem
2. Finding the core problem
3. Discovering why it is a problem
4. Exploration of feelings
5. Examining possible solutions and alternatives
6. Recognising their implications
7. Deciding on a course of action (including 'no-action').

The counsellor will only achieve an interview of this kind if he asks open-ended, pertinent questions. All the questioning words, like how, what, when, where, and why, enable the person to explore his own world, to clarify the

problem, to consider solutions and realise their implications.

Authoritarian people sometimes dismiss non-directive
counselling as a soft option, because they think it helps
people to avoid the truth, which may be harsh. But in fact,
the effective counsellor can ask questions which would
otherwise be avoided and, with sensitivity, can enter areas
which normally read 'keep out'.

Choosing the direction

Counselling is in some way an exploration, but it is necessary for the counsellor to steer the interview in the right
direction, that is, the direction that will lead to the resolution of the problem. But what is the 'right' direction?
There is no simple answer to this question, but it is a fact
that the counsellor takes the discussion into different
areas by his choice of question or response. He may move
down a path which turns out to be a dead end and the cost
may simply be the waste of a certain amount of time. On
the other hand, inappropriate questioning may result in
undue significance being attached to a problem of minor
importance, the resolution of which brings very little
benefit and leaves the real problem untouched.

The effective counsellor continually constructs mental
hypotheses and uses these as the basis for giving a direction to the discussion. The word 'hypothesis' – temporary
and tentative explanation which seems to fit the facts so
far, but which may be changed in the light of new and
different information – is important. The counsellor,
working in this way, is continually computing the facts
and feelings which he is hearing and perceiving, and tes-
ting them against the hypothesis he is forming. This leads
him to take a line of approach which enables the person
being counselled to explore and examine a particular
aspect of the situation and maybe gain new knowledge
and insight about himself in the process. The ensuing
conversation may then confirm the counsellor's
hypotheses and so enable him to go further down that

particular avenue. If however, the opposite happens, then
he rejects that idea and searches for another that is more
probable.

This skill of asking the right questions is directly
related to the counsellor's knowledge of human behaviour
and especially his awareness of the range of human
feelings and emotions. If he has an understanding of all
the kinds of factors which are likely to be contributing to
the problem, then he can construct wide-ranging
hypotheses which are more likely to be helpful and lead to
the core of the problem. If, on the other hand his general
understanding of human behaviour is narrow, then so will
be his hypotheses. This narrow approach is continually
revealed when people try to give an explanation of the
facts, and squeeze them into a limited and pre-conceived
view of how people behave. Such phrases as 'Of course, it
was a woman driver' or 'He's very introverted, like all
accountants' or 'Typical trade-union behaviour', are indi-
cative of this approach and say more about the speaker
than the situation they are trying to explain. The effective
counsellor will keep an open mind, being neither surprised by what he hears nor afraid to go into areas which
others may think are out of bounds.

SUMMARY

The effective counsellor helps his client explore and clarify his problems and find his own solutions. There are seven important aspects to successful counselling:

1. Listening

The kind of listening required by the counsellor is active rather than passive. This means not only encouraging the client to do most of the talking, but ensuring that he knows he is the centre of the counsellor's attention and interest.

2. Recognising the 'presenting problem'

The counsellor needs to recognise that the initial problem presented is rarely a full statement of the real problem. The client is likely to use a form of words which is generally acceptable and he will need encouragement from the counsellor to go further.

3. Finding the core problem

The core problem is the heart of the matter which is worrying the client. It always concerns his situation at the present time and usually involves his relationship with other people.

4. Recognising and admitting feelings

Effective counselling allows a person to explore and recognise the feelings associated with the problem.

5. Criticism

Criticism makes people feel threatened and they protect themselves by operating defence mechanisms. The result is that the counselling process stops, even though the ·interview may continue.

6. The problem-solving process

The counsellor should follow these stages as he helps the client deal with his problem:

   (a) Recognising the presenting problem
   (b) Finding the core problem
   (c) Discovering why it is a problem
   (d) Recognising and explaining feelings
   (e) Examining possible solutions and alternatives
   (f) Recognising their implications
   (g) Deciding on a course of action.

7. Influencing the direction

Even though the counsellor is trying not to lead his client down any pre-determined path, his every question and response will immediately give the conversation direction and emphasis. If he has a broad knowledge of human nature, his questions will direct the client towards greater self-understanding and an ability to select a course of action which is right for him.

4

Counselling and Performance Appraisal

Part of every manager's job must be to appraise the performance of his subordinates. This may happen after a particular assignment or project and, in many of the large auditing firms, for instance, a manager completes an assignment report for each person involved at the end of a particular audit. This is also happening more and more in computer software firms, where consultants are forming project teams to work with clients and the teams are appraised at the project's completion. But the most common method of appraisal is the Company Appraisal scheme where at regular intervals – usually once a year – the manager completes a performance assessment of his subordinates' work over the last period. Such an appraisal covers various aspects of work and may entail ticking boxes, marking five-point scales or simply writing an open-ended report. As well as this, many companies operate some sort of 'management by objective' scheme and use the targets that were agreed and set at the previous meeting as the measure for the actual achievement.

Trying to work all of these schemes can cause immense problems. Not least is the anxiety felt by managers when they have to hold an appraisal interview with someone who does not want it and with whom they have little sympathy or empathy. Another problem is the actual paper system. One sheet must go to the personnel department, one is retained by the manager, the subordinate is given a copy – but only of certain things! It is not unusual for the preparation and distribution of the paperwork to take up to 90 per cent of everyone's effort in these schemes, leaving only 10 per cent for the actual appraisal.

There can be only one way forward which is likely to prove effective. *An appraisal scheme must be client-centred.* That is, the primary task of appraisal must be to help the subordinate, and anything that hinders this should be modified or scrapped. Just as effective counselling requires a certain relationship, so an effective appraisal scheme can only operate within an appropriate organisational climate.

There are many reasons why organisations carry out performance appraisal, for instance:

– to provide knowledge of individual performance
– to plan for future promotions and successions
– to assess training and development needs
– to provide information for salary planning and special awards
– to contribute to corporate career planning and progression.

But the prime aim must be to help the person being appraised. This means that he should know exactly where he stands with his boss and within the company and can take appropriate action to build on his strengths and reduce his weaknesses. Not only is this in line with good human relations, it also has the practical result of contributing to the development of the organisation's most important asset – its people.

If the main purpose in appraising a person's performance is to contribute to their motivation and development, *appraisal must be linked with counselling*. If appraisal means evaluating an employee's worth, then counselling means communicating that information in such a way that the individual can use it positively. That being so, certain principles about an appraisal and counselling interview can be stated.

PRINCIPLES FOR AN APPRAISAL AND COUNSELLING INTERVIEW

1. Everything written should be shown and shared. This is probably the most important principle for the following reasons:

Secrecy breeds suspicion. Whilst the manager may feel he has good reason to keep certain facts or opinion hidden, his subordinate is bound to put the worst construction on this. Suspicion is the emotion most likely to destroy a counselling relationship. As well as this, it is vital for a subordinate to know the source of any criticism; nothing is more worrying than hearing one's boss say 'I gather that you have done so and so' without disclosing who has told him.

Elliott Jaques put this well:

This kind of behaviour is infuriating. It arouses feelings of contempt toward the manager for listening to tales from others, and scorn for the unknown others. Such reactions are not surprising since secret tale-bearing is a very paranoiagenic (fear-creating) act. Any organisation in which behaviour of this kind becomes rife is going to pieces: the behaviour is a powerful aid to the disintegration. *(A General Theory of Bureaucracy)*

There are frequently two aspects in appraisals which are
not communicated, and these relate to poor performance
and potential promotion.

With regard to poor performance, the secrecy reflects
the manager's own anxiety. How can he tell his subordinate that he is doing badly? The answer (which is easier
said than done) is that no-one can improve until they are
aware of their faults. And, of course, if this is dealt with in
a counselling manner, the manager himself may find that
he is part of the problem and so can become part of the
solution.

The usual argument for not communicating information regarding potential promotion to the subordinate is
that he will interpret it as a statement of fact and will be
very disappointed if it does not happen. On the other hand,
a person surely has a right to know how he is regarded by
his company and should also have plenty of time to consider a possible future promotion and the effect this may
have on him and his family. The manager must ensure
that the subordinate understands that the promotion is
not a certainty and that there are various factors which
might affect the final decision, especially the subordinate's continuing high performance.

How many companies have had the unhappy experience
of losing their best men because they were never told of
the company's high opinion of them?

Finally, if there is still something that the manager
feels he cannot communicate to his subordinate, then that
is probably a good enough reason for excluding it from the
appraisal report.

2. The appraisal report should be finalised in the presence
of the subordinate.

The main reason for this is that the subordinate should
know exactly what the completed document contains
before it goes on the file. The other reason is that if the
appraisal is communicated in a counselling interview,
new facts may arise which may alter the manager's view
and he may wish to change what he has already written.
The subordinate may also disagree with some parts of the

appraisal and if, at the end of the interview he still disagrees, he must have the opportunity to state his disagreement, which must be recorded.

A further point is that many schemes involve the subordinate's 'grandfather', i.e. the manager's manager, who will not necessarily see the subordinate, but will write a comment on the report, possibly following a discussion with the manager. Again, there seems no reason why the subordinate should not see these comments and he may even learn something from the views of a senior executive.

3. The subordinate should contribute a major part to the appraisal.

No-one knows the subordinate better than he knows himself, and in a counselling relationship with an encouraging manager, he can explore and assess his own performance. Self-appraisal is particularly effective in two areas. The first concerns the area of weak performance and in a supportive relationship individuals can be remarkably open and honest about themselves. The counselling manager enables his subordinate to examine these areas in an analytic rather than a critical way, and helps him discover courses of action which will lead to improvement. Where these facts have to be written into an appraisal report, the manager will choose words which demonstrate the subordinate's self-insight and which therefore do not become incriminating or damning. Rather, they reveal the qualities of self-knowledge and become positive factors in the overall appraisal.

The other effective area resulting from self-appraisal is career progression. Managers are likely to see a subordinate's future in terms of what has happened to other people in their department and, especially in terms of their own career progression. By giving his subordinate the opportunity to talk about his aspirations, he may well discover aims and ambitions of which he himself was totally unaware. This may enable him to plan work experience and specific training for the subordinate, or at least note these hopes on the appraisal report, so that central personnel are aware of them.

THE DYNAMICS OF AN APPRAISAL/COUN-SELLING INTERVIEW

Most managers and their subordinates feel apprehensive about taking part in an appraisal and counselling interview. Harold J. Leavitt has tried to explain this by dividing manager's styles into two major categories – 'direct' and 'relational'. 'Direct' styles are used by get-it-done, task-oriented people who compete to win. 'Relational' styles, in contrast are used by managers and always involve relationships with other people. They help, support and back up other people and often get their feelings of achievement by contributing to the success of others. Using these two concepts, Leavitt writes about performance appraisals:

> Performance appraisal systems offer a clear example of direct/relational dilemma of modern management. Almost every organisation uses some form of comparative performance evaluation scheme. But the words 'comparative' and 'performance' and 'evaluation' are all direct-style words. Extreme relational-type managers don't like to be compared or evaluated or to have their performance measured. They prefer to 'accept' and 'support' and 'help' one another. The very concept of individual performance evaluation presumes individuals competing with one another to achieve individual rewards. That may be why both managers and managed are so universally uncomfortable with performance evaluation procedures. They violate our relational side. The best that such evaluation schemes engender is a love-hate ambivalence. Performance appraisal programmes don't founder because they use the wrong forms or the wrong categories; they get into trouble because both honest appraisers and realistic appraisees hate to confront what is almost inevitably an uncomfortable – indeed unhuman – evaluation interview. So they either skip it or muck it up. (*Organizational Dynamics*)

It is useful to analyse some of the emotional factors

which may be present on both sides at such an interview and which will affect the meeting to a greater or lesser extent.

The manager – positive feelings

To be helpful and understanding By virtue of his greater experience and superior position in the organisation, the manager may be justified in feeling that he has knowledge and understanding which will help his subordinate. He may also feel that he has a good understanding of people's behaviour, learnt both from his working experience and some theoretical knowledge of the behavioural sciences. The danger here is that the manager, seeing his subordinate encounter problems similar to those he himself has experienced, will offer solutions which worked for him. To be helpful and understanding in a positive way, the manager must recognise that his subordinate is an autonomous human being with a complex and unique personality, and that his problems require their own, individual solutions.

To be kind and tolerant Most managers would like to see themselves as kind and tolerant – the sort of boss who is liked and respected by his staff. However, this should not lead to a policy of appeasement: the manager who is frightened to point out the truth so colludes with his subordinate's poor performance or fantasy. Feelings of kindness are used positively when the manager helps the subordinate to see the facts of the situation and to come to grips with reality.

For instance, for a manager to allow a subordinate to continue to think that his performance is good and that promotion and salary increases will come in the future, when he knows full well that this is unlikely, is not an act of kindness. Neither is it kind, as occasionally happens, for the manager to withhold knowledge of future promotion, giving the subordinate a surprise at the last minute like an unexpected present. In this case, the subordinate is helped by knowing of the promotion as soon as possible so that he has time to make the necessary adjustments, both physical and psychological.

The manager – negative feelings

Fear of the interview itself. The thought of carrying out an appraisal and counselling interview can make a manager very anxious and these anxieties are based on a variety of fears. The first fear concerns the interview itself – will he do it well? Will his subordinate see him as a fool, unable to cope with the situation and letting it get out of hand, with unforeseen results? Does he understand the actual purpose of the appraisal scheme? What will happen if the subordinate asks him questions to which he doesn't know the answer? All these fears are an inevitable part of counselling and are part of the price a manager pays for trying to build effective relationships with his subordinates. They can only be diminished by practice and the more interviews a manager carries out, the less these fears will hinder him.

Counselling training, where people have an opportunity to practise facing up to these fears and overcoming them, is very useful.

Fear of unleashing powerful emotions. Because performance appraisal is such a personal activity, the manager may fear that the subordinate has extremely strong feelings concerning his work and concerning his boss. He may fear that one inappropriate word will unleash a whole range of emotions which would be highly embarrassing and difficult to control. However, whilst the subordinate may have strong feelings, it is rare for emotions to come bursting out like lava from a volcano. The opposite is more usual, that is, people are reticent about their feelings and usually need a lot of encouragement before they will express them. The way to reduce this fear is to build up a relationship with the subordinate in which the expression of feelings plays a natural part.

Envying the subordinate. Envy can be described as 'the angry feeling that another person possesses and enjoys something desirable – the envious impulse being to take it away or spoil it' (M. Klein, 1957). On the face of it, the manager has little reason to envy his subordinate. After all, he has a higher position, a larger salary, etc. But there may be other things he envies – such as his youth and health and the greater opportunities he seems to have for future success and achievement.

Perhaps the most common cause for envy lies in the subordinate's qualifications. Many managers who are not graduates, but who hold responsible posts, are deeply envious of graduates and consequently look for ways to devalue them – 'bloody graduates, they think the world owes them a living'. Or as an engineering director once said, 'No graduate's any use to me until he's worn a pair of overalls and got his hands dirty!'

Envy can also lead a manager to hinder his subordinates efforts to prevent him succeeding; or else to belittle any success he does have. The more the manager can acknowledge to himself that he has these feelings, the more he can control them and minimise their negative effect.

The subordinate – positive feelings

To be liked and accepted. One of the most basic desires in everyone is to be liked, and even loved, and accepted for what one is, warts and all. Because of the very nature of their relationship, the subordinate places a special value on the boss's estimation of him. Whilst this is a natural feeling, it can lead to overdependence and to a desire to please at any cost. In appraising and counselling, the interview can sometimes be used by a subordinate as a confessional, and he waits to hear the words of absolution. If the boss colludes in such fantasies, the subordinate is encouraged in his feelings of dependence and may even say such things as 'Tell me what to do. I'll accept your opinion. After all, you're the boss!' An overriding wish to be liked. leads the subordinate to deny the awkward and difficult parts of his nature. But although they might cause friction, it is better that they should be faced, than be sacrificed on the altar of his boss's affection.

To get help with problems. It has been stressed that good counselling helps a person solve his own problems. A manager can also give his subordinate support and sympathy. Of course, not every appraisal interview will require this sort of approach, and many subordinates will have no serious problems at work or at home. However, if a counselling relationship exists, the subordinate knows that his boss is interested in him, and will listen to him because he really cares. The interivew can then fulfill a need which might otherwise not be met.

The subordinate – negative feelings

Fear of criticism and punishment. An appraisal interview aims to evaluate all areas of performance, both strong and weak, successes and failures. The greatest fear in the mind of any subordinate at an appraisal interview is that his performance will be criticised and, like a prisoner in the dock, he will be found guilty. The fear of criticism is linked to the wish to be liked by the boss, and concern for salary and career; there may even be a fear of being sacked. Whilst legislation now prevents unlawful dismissal, there is no doubt that a manager can affect his subordinate's future in all sorts of ways and make his daily life extremely unpleasant. The only way in which these fears can be allayed is by building a relationship between manager and subordinate in which poor performance is discussed as it happens and the manager shows himself to be fair and trustworthy in his day-to-day behaviour.

SUMMARY

A. Every manager has to appraise the performance of his subordinates and this usually involves a formal interview. Company appraisal schemes can be very time-consuming and if they are to be useful, they must be client-centred. This means that appraisal interviews must be linked with counselling, so that the subordinate can use the appraisal information positively. An appraisal and counselling interview is more likely to be effective if the following points are borne in mind.

1. The manager should show his subordinate everything that he has written about him and share it with him. Anything else breeds suspicion. This is especially true of poor performance, and it is the only way in which improvements are likely to be made.
2. The appraisal report should be finalised in the presence of the subordinate. This allows him to know exactly what is being placed on file and provides him with the opportunity, if he wishes, to record any disagreement he may have with the report.
3. The subordinate should contribute a large part of the appraisal. Self-appraisal is particularly effective in two areas:

    (a) Poor performance. In a counselling relationship people can exercise self-criticism, which is a prerequisite of change and improvement.

    (b) Career progression. Self-appraisal allows a person to explore his career aspirations so that appropriate training and work experience can be planned, to the benefit of the individual and the organisation.

B. Both manager and subordinate can feel anxious and apprehensive about an appraisal interview. An analysis of the emotional dynamics in these situations can help both parties to understand the reasons for this and to cope better.

1. The manager's positive feelings.

(a) The manager wants to be helpful and under-standing, but may be inclined to offer advice too closely related to his own experience. He will offer positive help when he recognises his subordinate as a unique indi-vidual.

(b) He wants to be kind and tolerant and to be liked by his staff. But he must not let these feelings prevent him from pointing out the reality of the situation, even if this is painful.

2. The manager's negative feelings.

(a) The manager may be fearful of the interview itself and worry that he will make a mess of it. This is the price he pays for building a strong relationship with his subordinates and these fears will diminish with practice.

(b) He may fear that the interview will get very emotional and that the subordinate may express strong hostile feeling towards him. These fears can be reduced by developing a relationship with his subordinate in which the expression of feelings is a normal part of that relationship.

(c) The manager may have feelings of envy towards his subordinate concerning his youth, health, qualifications or career opportunities. He needs to ack-nowledge these and not let them influence his behaviour by belittling or hindering his subordinate's progress and achievements.

3. The subordinate's positive feelings.

(a) The subordinate wants to be liked by his boss and receive his approbation. But he must not let this desire lead him to deny the awkward parts of himself and take up a dependent attitude.

(b) The wish to get help with any problems he has can, with a counselling relationship, become a realistic part of the interview.

4.The subordinate's negative feelings.

The most likely emotion which the subordinate will feel is fear of being criticised for his work or behaviour, and unless this fear is allayed, the interview will achieve

nothing. Only the manager can do this through a counselling relationship which shows that he is fair and
trustworthy.

REFERENCES

Jaques, E., *A General Theory of Bureaucracy,* Heinemann,
1976
Klein, M., *Envy and Gratitude,* Tavistock Publications,
1957, p.6
Leavitt, H. J. and Lipman-Brown, J., 'A Case for the
Relational Manager,' *Organizational Dynamics,* Summer,
1980

5

Counselling is very much to do with the ways in which people relate and behave with one another. The important relationship within which counselling takes place has been characterised by such words as 'encouragement', 'trust' and 'openness'. No doubt every manager and subordinate would like to have this kind of relationship. However, business pressures and personality conflicts can all work against this ideal. There is often mistrust and suspicion between people, resulting in criticism and fear which can make counselling difficult if not impossible; neither party plans it that way, but the same fraught situations occur time and time again, leading to rows and bad feelings.

An analysis of the mechanisms that operate when people try to communicate their thoughts and feelings to each other may be helpful.

There are many theories put forward by psychologists to explain these matters, and all have their followers, but few managers have the time or inclination to study such writers as Freud or Jung. Recently, however, a method of analysing behaviour has been developed which has the virtues of being simple and easily communicated. This is called 'Transactional Analysis' and was developed by the late Eric Berne, author of the bestselling book *Games People Play*. Transactional Analysis has something very specific to say about effective counselling (although its aims are far wider than this), and many managers have found the theory easy to absorb and to relate to their own experience. It is therefore described below in some detail.

EGO-STATES

It is common experience that the same person can behave very differently at different times. A person who is rational and able to consider calmly all the aspects of a problem may, on occasion, become angry and highly emotional. A person may behave quite differently at home and at work. When these changes in behaviour are extreme, it may even be commented that 'he seemed to be a different person'.

Transactional Analysis explains this by saying that everyone is always in one of three possible 'ego-states'. 'Ego-state' simply means 'the state I am in' and includes the language and tone of voice we use, the emotions and feelings we have and our physical appearance and stance. The three ego-states are called Parent, Adult and Child and we move from one to the other continuously as we react to the different situations in which we find ourselves.

Parent

The Parent ego-state contains all the values and morals we have been taught since birth. It contains our standards for living and enables us to say what is right or wrong; what is good or bad. These values come from our actual parents: they were the chief influence on our behaviour and their words and actions moulded our early years. Their words and attitudes are permanently stored in our minds and can be switched on rather like a tape recorder. The stern look, the wagging finger, the use of such words as 'Never let me catch you doing that again!' all indicate that someone is in their Parent ego-state. But our parents were loving and nurturing as well as critical, and this side of our experience is also present in the Parent ego-state, showing itself in caring and comforting behaviour and such words as 'Don't worry, I'll take care of it'.

Here are some characteristics of the Parent ego-state:

Words   Don't, never, always, well done, splendid
Voice   Stern, critical, angry, comforting, concerned
Gestures   Frown, wag finger, arm around shoulder
Attitude   Authoritarian, judgemental, caring

Adult

The Adult ego-state is the rational, unemotional way we have of behaving which deals with the reality of what is actually happening. It contains all the information, knowledge and skills we have accumulated and can deal with facts and figures, solve problems, consider different courses of action and compute their possible outcomes and implications. Because of this, the Adult is the state in which we learn and in which we can choose to take new and different approaches.

Some characteristics of the Adult ego-state are:

Words   How? What? Why? When? Is it practical?
Voice   Calm, even
Gestures   Alert, thoughtful
Attitude   Analytic, evaluative, attentive, constructive

Child

The Child ego-state contains all the emotions and feelings as they were experienced in childhood. At birth, all we have is our Child, laughing or crying, and this Natural Child is still a part of ourselves, self-centred and demanding, spontaneous and uninhibited, loving and fun-loving. However, this Natural Child is rapidly affected by the attitudes of parents and other influential people in the process of socialisation, resulting in the Adapted Child. The Adapted Child results from the rewards and punishments given by the parents as, for instance, the infant learns that it is more likely to get what it wants by asking politely rather than screaming for it.

Here are some characteristics of the Child ego-state:

Words Want, can't, wish, hope, please, thank you, I wonder . . ., wouldn't it be nice if . . .
Voice Giggling, whining, excited, whispering, pleading
Gestures Spontaneous, sad, happy, whimsical
Attitude Joking, ashamed, creative, manipulative, sulky, curious, dependent, scared

All three ego-states are vital to effective living and none is 'better' than the other. The important things to realise is that in communicating with other people, each state brings different results and has important implications for work and relationships. This way of looking at behaviour is called Transactional Analysis, and based on these ideas a person can be represented by three circles in the following way:

Basically, when we are in the Parent – we believe; when we are in the Adult – we think; and when we are in the Child – we feel.

This simple model of behaviour provides a useful way of analysing any transaction which takes place between people. Anyone starting a conversation must be speaking from either their Parent, Adult or Child ego-state and the other person's reply must also come from one of these.

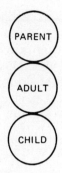

Here is a simple example:

Manager: Don't ever let me catch you writing a report like this again. It's a load of rubbish!
Subordinate: I'm very sorry, I only had two days to finish it. But it won't happen again.

Clearly, the manager is in the Parent ego-state criticising the report in very general terms, and treating his subordinate like a naughty boy.

The subordinate, not unnaturally, replies from his Child ego-state and, because he feels guilty, apologises and promises to do better in the future, just as a small boy might respond to an angry father.

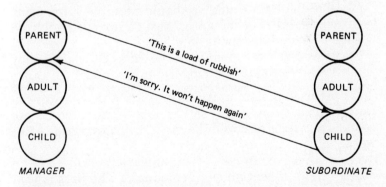

However, in the same situation, the exchange might be as follows:

Manager: John, the boss is playing hell over that report

and I'm scared we'll get clobbered. Could you re-write bits of it, just enough to make him happy? I'm up to my eyes in work.
Subordinate: Don't you worry, I'll take care of it. What you want is a nice cup of coffee.

In this case, the manager is in his Child, frightened of his boss's anger and behaving in a very dependent way on his subordinate. The subordinate responds from his Parent, comforting him like a kindly father, indicating that he will take care of everything.

Or, the exchange might be:

Manager: John, I think we should examine your report in more detail. For instance, those figures you quote on page 3, where did they come from?
Subordinate: I got them from the Sales Office, but they may be out of date. I'll ring Peter and check.

Here the manager is in his Adult, calm and unemotional and getting down to the facts. The subordinate replies from his Adult and the result will be some effecitve work.

From these examples, two important principles of human communication can be deduced. The first is that the person who begins speaking and initiates the transaction is (unconsciously) trying to 'hook' the complementary ego-state of the other. In the first example above, the manager in his critical Parent hooks the guilty Child of

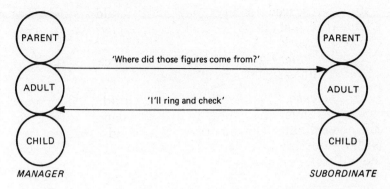

his subordinate. In the second example, the manager in his dependent and scared Child hooks the comforting Parent of the subordinate. In the final example, the calm, problem-solving Adult of the manager connects with the Adult of the subordinate. As we shall see, not every transaction is complementary, but many transactions involve Parent-Child ego-states or else they are Adult-Adult.

The second principle is that in these kinds of complementary transactions the communication can go on indefinitely, although the quality of the conversation may not be high. For instance, many managers have a Parent-Child relationship with their subordinates and they both work comfortably in these ego-states over many years.

Of course, life at work (or at home) is never a series of smooth transactions. People get angry or upset, rows occur and relationships get damaged. It is in this area of bad communications that TA can provide an analytical tool to explain what is happening. Put simply, communications stop and bad situations arise when the transactions cut across each other. Here is a classic work situation to illustrate this:

Manager: (threateningly) You're responsible for getting these budgets. If anything goes wrong, I'll hold you responsible! (Parent)
Subordinate: How dare you speak to me like that. Apologise at once! (Parent)

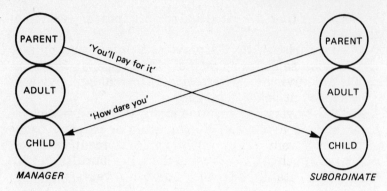

Both people are in their Parent, one angry and threatening, the other equally angry and full of righteous indignation. Each is treating the other like a child and so their transactions cross each other. The scene is all set for a really good row.

Here is another example of crossed transactions:

Secretary: Please help me find that letter from Head Office. If I've lost it the boss will kill me!
Colleague: Don't blame me. I haven't got it.

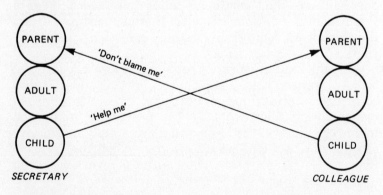

In this instance, the secretary is in her Child, but her friend also replies from her Child and so the transactions are crossed.

Just reading these examples one can imagine the tensions that inevitably result from these exchanges and the 'atmosphere' that is created and remains possibly for some time.

To summarise so far, TA provides a unique and simple way to analyse and understand what happens when two people are having a conversation and exchanging views. Two important points emerge.

Firstly, in every conversation we have, there are always three options available. We can start or respond from either our Parent, Adult or Child and the results will be different in each case. Because of the behavioural patterns we have all established over a number of years, many of our reactions have become automatic and seem inevitable. For instance, if a subordinate makes a mistake it may seem the natural thing for the manager to reprimand him and behave in the Critical Parent. Likewise, if we are criticised, we usually apologise and make our excuses (from the Child) or else start a fight (from the Parent). But these ideas from TA show that this is neither inevitable nor desirable. It is the realisation of these potential choices with the resulting increase in personal freedom that makes TA so stimulating and effective.

The second point is that poor relationships, rows and unpleasant feelings between people can usually be explained by analysing the conversations that take place and seeing where, in TA terms, the lines cross. Understanding this does not immediately result in sweetness and light, but it does mean that on the next occasion, a different approach can be considered, which may prove to be more effective and constructive.

WORKING IN THE ADULT

It should now be obvious that effective counselling will only occur when both manager and subordinate are operating in their Adult ego-state. This is not to deny the importance of either the Parent or the Child. But the Adult is the appropriate and necessary condition for doing counselling work. When we operate from the Adult we behave as rational, unemotional people, in touch with reality and acting in an alert and thoughtful manner. Consider, as an example, the following statement made by a subordinate at an appraisal and counselling interview:

What really concerns me is my future prospects. I'm 51, a departmental manager and I've been in this position for the last six years, before you became my boss. I do my job efficiently, but I ought to get promotion soon if I'm going to make the grade. I'd like to ask you straight out – when will I get promotion?

This kind of statement puts any manager in a very delicate situation and there are a variety of ways in which he can answer. Here are some possible responses, based on the different ego-states he may be in:

A. *Critical Parent*
You know very well that these decisions are made by the central personnel department. The more you keep on about it the less you are helping yourself. What you've got to do is show me, over the next six months that you're capable of being promoted. That cock-up you made last week didn't exactly inspire me with confidence.

B. *Nurturing Parent*
Look Fred, you've nothing to worry about. You know I take care of all the boys in my department. When have I ever let you down? I'll put in a good word for you in the right place, never fear. Meanwhile, keep your chin up and things will come right in the end. After all, like my old father used to say – it will all be the same in 100 years!

C. *Child*
How should I know? Nobody tells me anything around here. They must think I've nothing better to do than to spend all my time on staff matters. It's not fair. I wish personnel would get up off its backside and do some work for a change. Why don't you go and ask them? Not

that you'll get a decision out of that lot. But I don't know why you're worried. Look at me! I'm five years older than you and I don't know whay they're planning for me. And the wife's not all that well.

Each of these responses would cause a different reaction in the subordinate. To response A, the subordinate is likely to feel sad and depressed and worried that in some undefined way his performance is below standard. Because the criticism is so vague, he has nothing specific to work on other than the comment about the incident last week. He may well latch on to this and respond with a string of excuses (Child) or try and start a fight (Parent).

The subordinate may feel a little comforted and reassured by the friendly words of the manager who gives response B. But he will recognise that what is being said is 'flannel', a smokescreen of words that are easily said but which on analysis, mean absolutely nothing. They may sell serve the manager's purpose, which is to move on quickly from this embarrassing situation. Unless the subordinate has a great deal of courage and determination, he will accept the reassurance and agree with the manager's words. But, of course, nothing has changed and he will leave the interview with his problems and worries unresolved.

If the manager gives response C, the subordinate is likely to feel confused and baffled. After all, if his boss apparently doesn't know about his own future, how can he possibly counsel and advise his subordinate? They apparently have a common enemy in the personnel department and the outcome could be a game called 'Ain't it Awful'. However, the manager has signalled loudly that he is in his Child by the way he refers to his sick wife. The most likely outcome is that the subordinate will respond with sympathy, hoping the wife will soon be better, and so on, i.e. moving into the Nurturing Parent.

These three responses have one thing in common: they all prevent effective counselling. They are all likely to engage the subordinate's Parent or Child so that the work of analysing and resolving his problem is made impossible. It could be argued that this is in fact the manager's motive, because it enables him to avoid facing up to a delicate issue.

The manager's *Adult* responses could be something like this:

I understand your concern, Fred. Looking back over your time in this department, can you think of any reasons why you may have been overlooked for promotion?

OR

To be honest with you, I'm not sure. You see, when I put in my reports recommending promotions, I must be fair to the other people in our department. Take John and Terry for instance. They've both got full membership of the institute and I know you're only an associate member. That makes very little difference in your present position but I think it must be taken into account for higher level work. Are you unhappy in your job? You seem to run your department well. Perhaps you're feeling a bit stale?

OR

I'm interested to know why you want promotion so badly. You run your department well and you're at the top of your salary scale. Promotion won't give you that much extra, especially after tax. What are the advantages you hope to get?

The reader can no doubt think up a great number of other Adult responses, and each will have the same effect. Because they are in the Adult and ask a question, they are most likely to get an Adult response from the subordinate. The result is that he will be enabled to analyse his own problem further and gain more self-insight. In the above case, the solution appears to be a realisation of the fact that he will not get promotion and an understanding of the reasons why. If the counselling manager can facilitate this recognition and self-acceptance in his subordinate, then he will have provided real help.

CONCLUSION

No one can begin to solve his problems until he is able to face up to the realities of his situation. This essential and sometimes painful process can only come about when the individual is in his Adult, realising all the facts and their implications and as a result deciding on some appropriate course of action. The effective counsellor facilitates this process by being himself in his Adult and asking questions which allow the subordinate to explore his own world. The outcome is not only the resolution of the problem, but also a person who is developing greater self-insight and who is growing psychologically.

SUMMARY

Effective counselling requires an open and trusting relationship between the counsellor and his client. However,
pressures at work can cause hostility and suspicion between a manager and his subordinate which makes counselling extremely difficult. Transactional Analysis provides a way of understanding the mechanisms of interpersonal communication and suggests ways of behaviour
which are likely to be beneficial for counselling.

A. People are always in one of three ego-states: Parent,
Adult or Child.

> *Parent* — The Parent ego-state consists of the values
> and morals we received from our parents. It is the state
> in which we are critical and judgemental, typified by
> the wagging finger and the stern rebuke. It is also the
> state in which, like our parents, we can be loving and
> nurturing, taking care of people.
> *Adult* — In the Adult ego-state, we are unemotional,
> dealing rationally with the facts that concern us. We
> use all the information, knowledge and skills we pos-
> sess, and this is the appropriate state for learning and
> problem-solving.
> *Child* — In the Child ego-state we experience all the
> emotions and feelings as they were experienced in
> childhood. These feelings typically involve sadness, fun,
> rebelliousness, creativity, fear and dependency.

All three states are part of normal behaviour; the skill lies
in choosing the state which is appropriate to the situation.

B. In any conversation, each person is speaking and
responding from one of their three ego-states. As long as
these transactions are complementary, i.e. Parent-
Parent, Parent-Child, Adult-Adult, Child-Child or
Child-Parent, communication can proceed smoothly. But
communication breaks down when the transactions cross,

and this is usually when both persons speak from their Parent and direct their words to the other's Child.

C. Using Transactional Analysis theory, it becomes obvious that effective counselling will only happen when both the counsellor and his client are working in their Adult ego-state. The Adult enables both parties to look at the facts of the situation and rationally examine possible solutions and their implications. It also allows the client to choose new courses of action and new ways of behaviour, resulting in learning and growth.

REFERENCES

Berne, E., *Games People Play,* Grove Press Inc., 1964; Penguin Books, 1968.

6

Journey Into
Life-space

Counselling is a very private and personal activity. It usually concerns only two people, both of whom are trying to come to grips with reality. The counsellor is concerned with the reality of the person he is attempting to help as well as the problem which he presents. Who is he? How does he think? What sort of a person is he?

The better the counsellor can recognise and accept the fact that the person he is dealing with is different from anybody else in the world, the more genuine help he will bring to the situation. But this can also be threatening because meeting strangers can create anxiety, and the recognition that someone is different from ourselves can be frightening.

To overcome these fears and anxieties and to avoid the hard work of getting to know someone, there is a tendency to put labels on people and then to start dealing with the label – not the person.

The labels we use come from powerful memories of past experiences. For instance, our early family lives are bound to be strong in our memories and especially the roles of our parents. It is likely therefore that many managers who are middle-aged tend to see their younger subordinates as their children and treat them accordingly. This is not always done consciously, but when counselling, the handiest label to put on the subordinate is 'son' or 'daughter', and the manager then proceeds to play the wise patriarch or the stern father. However, if he wishes to play the part of counsellor, he must throw away the 'child' label and attempt to meet the real person who is confronting him. (This can be a two-way process: the subordinate may come to a counselling meeting with the expectation of meeting a father-figure.)

Other labels we use may be based on myth and folklore concerning people's appearance. Eyes too close together indicate untrustworthiness or even, in some people's mind, criminality. Eyebrows that meet in the middle are a sign of temper – as is red hair. A straight nose indicates honesty, and so on. I even heard someone describe a candidate after an interview as 'having the long upper lip of the humorist!'

As well as individual features, a person's general appearance can sometimes remind us of someone else and this may affect the way we behave to the new person.

All of these labelling techniques are part of normal behaviour and providing the counsellor is aware of them, they should not hinder effective counselling.

But one technique of labelling which can be detrimental to counselling is that of stereotyping. This can happen particularly at work when certain functions are thought to attract similar personalities. Perhaps accountants and finance people are most likely to be stereotyped – 'They're all the same. Narrow minded, unimaginative, work to the rules, and are cold and aloof'. Sales people are often labelled as hearty extroverts who fiddle their expenses, enjoy a lunchtime drink and play golf every Friday. This kind of labelling can simply be a bit of fun, just as stereotyping the Welsh or the English, the Germans or the French has its place in good-humoured banter. But it is more serious when people are only allowed to play the stereotype. For instance, in a meeting, an accountant might have something to say about the people-side of the business but his view may be completely discounted – 'After all, he's only the accountant.' Similarly, academics may be stereotyped as ineffective people, living in an ivory tower and not in the real world, who are more at home with books than with people.

As has been said, this process of labelling is something that everyone does to avoid the hard work of really getting to know an individual. In many circumstances it may not matter very much, although in its extreme forms it can be highly dangerous, resulting in racial prejudice and the irrational dislike of large groups of people and even nations.

But for the counsellor, any labelling leads to ineffectiveness. His job, as far as possible is to free his mind from any comparisons he may be tempted to make, and to recognise the uniqueness of the person he is meeting, as if this was the first person he has ever met. With this attitude, counselling can become a genuine encounter where fresh attitudes and new beginnings can emerge and where change becomes a real possibility – for both parties.

Counselling involves an encounter. For the counsellor, this means trying to enter the private and personal world of the other person in order to be of help. One way of describing this is to use the idea of 'life-space'.

LIFE-SPACE

The concept of 'life-space' was first put forward by the great psychologist, Kurt Lewin. He was trying to show how all behaviour is based in the present moment or, in the phrase he coined, 'the here and now'. He illustrated this with the diagram below, representing the life space of a child.

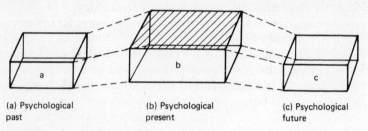

(a) Psychological   (b) Psychological   (c) Psychological
past   present   future

Life-space of a child (Based on Lewin)

Life-space of a child

This diagram represents a child's life-space at the present time. The child has a large part of this space concerned with what is actually happening now, including all his feelings and emotions (the 'psychological present'). But his behaviour is also affected by his past experiences, although for a child, this is relatively short (the 'psychological past'). At the same time, his present situation is also affected by his hopes, fears and expectations of what the future may hold (the 'psychological future'). Any action which the child now takes is in some way affected by these three aspects of his life-space.

The adult equally has a 'life-space' but it is different from that of the child because of the greater psychological time perspectives. As the diagram shows, the adult, in contrast to the child, has not only a longer past available for recall, but is also able to imagine a more distant future.

In other words, every individual exists in a psychological field of forces which, for him, determines and limits his behaviour. This 'force-field' is another idea of Lewin's and is based on theories from physics, which refer to magnetism and electricity. For instance, the space around a magnet is called a magnetic field and consists of invisible lines of force. This is easily proved by placing a sheet of paper over a magnet and then sprinkling iron filings on to the paper. The filings immediately take up a particular pattern, revealing the magnetic field. More importantly, it is the interaction of these force-fields, which result in the output of electric motors and generators.

The analogy to human behaviour is clear. Every individual has a psychological force-field around him which determines and limits his behaviour, and that is what Lewin called the 'life-space'. When one or more persons meet, their fields of force interact and the result is shown in their actual behaviour.

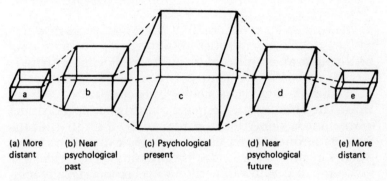

(a) More distant

(b) Near psychological past

(c) Psychological present

(d) Near psychological future

(e) More distant

Life-space of an adult (Based on Lewin)

LIFE-SPACE AND COUNSELLING

When these ideas are used in relation to counselling, they illuminate the counselling process and point to effective ways of operating.

1. Entering the life-space

It becomes clear that the first thing the counsellor must do is to gain entry into the life-space of the person being counselled. Short of psychological violence, there is no way in which such an entry can be forced. The door into another's private world is a barrier to be removed. Just as everyone develops physical ways of defending themselves

from unwanted intruders, so people develop psychological defences which prevent their inner selves from being revealed and violated.

The counsellor must create a climate of trust in which the person being counselled voluntarily opens the door of his life-space and welcomes the counsellor in. If there is already a good relationship between the two, this process will happen easily and counselling starts to progress. However, if the relationship is strained or simply does not exist (i.e. they only meet infrequently) then it will take more time for the counsellor to establish himself as trustworthy, competent and non-threatening. When this fails to happen, the counselling interview becomes totally ineffective. The counsellor makes no connection with the other person who puts all his energy into defending his inner life from a possible attack.

2. Behaviour within the life-space

Having access to an individual's private world is a privilege, and the counsellor, once he is invited into the other person's life-space, must respect this confidence. This is why criticism is so damaging to the counselling process. Criticism is essentially judging someone against one's own standards and pronouncing that their behaviour or performance is below these standards. This is an abuse of the counselling situation and offends against the autonomy of the individual. When it is done in the name of performance improvement and from the power position of superior to subordinate, it is even more objectionable.

Criticism will also inevitably stop the counselling process. Feeling criticised means feeling threatened and anyone who feels threatened when counselled immediately ejects the counsellor from their life-space. This can be compared with a visitor who is welcomed into a house and made at home, but who then starts to criticise the furniture or the decorations. Such a person will be asked to leave as soon as possible, and rightly so.

3. Exploring the life-space

The counsellor's role is to focus on the other person in order that he may be helped to focus on his problem. For the counsellor, this means that having gained the person's confidence, he can help him explore his life-space. This might seem a strange thing to suggest, for it could be argued that everyone knows themselves and does not require a tour of self-discovery. But the counsellor can help in three particular ways.

Firstly, people tend to push unpleasant facts and memories to the back of their mind and then do their best to forget about them. A skilled counsellor can help someone to 'remember' things which they would sooner forget but which may have a bearing on the current problem.

Secondly, the counsellor can help the person to see things from a different angle, just as an unusual camera shot can give new insights into a well known object.

Thirdly, the counsellor can help the person to consider possible outcomes and implications of certain courses of action. This might be done by asking the question 'What do you think will happen if you do so and so?' To which the answer may well be, 'I never thought of that!' Perhaps that is the skill of the counsellor in a nutshell: to get a person to consider an aspect of the problem which they would not otherwise have done.

4. Dealing with emotions and feelings

The life-space of an individual is, by definition, highly
subjective, dealing with the world as that person experiences it. But the world is experienced not only in terms of
facts and events but also in terms of emotions and feelings.
(Someone has said that at any time we feel sad, mad, glad
or bad!) Any problem brought for counselling will have
feelings associated with it and these may be weak or
strong. Sometimes the main component of the problem is
an emotion such as strong feelings of love or anger
towards someone which cannot be expressed. Some people
are closely in touch with their feelings and can express
them openly and clearly. Others appear to be dissociated
from their feelings, and are not able to express them or
appear not to know that they have any. Many people find
it difficult to show their feelings, perhaps because as children they were discouraged from doing so. In effective
counselling, the counsellor provides the opportunity for
the person to express their feelings, and this often helps
both parties to focus on the important issues. Any problem
causes feelings, such as anxiety, worry, fear or apprehen-
sion, and the stronger they are felt the greater must be the
problem. People generally welcome and value the opportunity to talk about their feelings and a simple question
like 'How does that make you feel?' is often sufficient.
There is a side-benefit in that the expression of feelings,
especially if they have been bottled-up for a long time,
brings genuine relief and can have a strongly therapeutic
effect.

5. The life-space, reality and fantasy

A person's life-space is the world as that individual sees it.
However, each person exists in the real world and must be
able to react with and respond to the other 'realities' of
people and events outside themselves. But because the
reality of the external world may be harsh, everyone finds
ways to minimise this harshness by fantasies, in which

they indulge privately in the game of 'let's pretend'. (Kurt Lewin gave this aspect of the life-space the interesting name of 'irreality'.)

People use fantasy in a variety of ways. For instance, the facts of a past event may be re-arranged so that the person, in relating a particular incident, appears to have a more important role in what happened. Or else it may be that the re-arrangement allows the person to be blameless. This is frequently demonstrated by people describing a road accident: it is always the other person's fault. This is different from lying: it represents what the person wishes had happened.

Some people act on fantasies of what the future will be, based on a selective arrangement of the facts. For instance, a man may come to believe that he is bound to be promoted when his superior retires and he may tell his wife and friends that it is a fact. He may even increase his spending on the basis of this belief. Of course, when he fails to get promotion, the reality of the situation will cause him a great deal of unhappiness.

Perhaps the most common area of fantasy is that of self-perception. How do I see myself? Am I brilliant, capable and successful or else a failure and incompetent? There can be no 'right' answer to these questions, because they are internal questions and people swing from optimism to pessimism.

Everybody has fantasies and no doubt they contribute to living a healthy and enjoyable life. Perhaps one sign of 'abnormality' is when someone is dominated by their fantasies to such an extent that they lose touch with reality. It is the counsellor's job to see that discussion of the problem and any solutions offered are based on fact. This means ensuring that the client understands what has really happened in the past to cause the problem and realises the implications of the solutions he is considering. The more that the client can examine the actual situation, the more likely he is to discover his own realistic solutions. Ineffective counselling results when the counsellor fails to challenge a fantasy ('Are you sure that's true?') or actually colludes with it.

SOLUTIONS THAT FIT THE LIFE-SPACE

Because life-space is unique to each individual person, any solution to a problem must be tailor-made to fit that space. This is why other people's suggestions are usually discarded or, when accepted, frequently turn out to be inappropriate or even disastrous. Such suggestions are based on another viewpoint and different experience; the words that every counsellor should avoid are 'if I were you'. The appropriate and realistic solution must fit into the overall behaviour pattern of the individual and be congruent with his personality. This is why the counsellor should at all times be considerate of the other person's feelings and realise that any direct advice or guidance demanding a change of long-held beliefs is likely to be rejected.

ON LEAVING THE LIFE-SPACE

Bringing a counselling interview to an end requires as much skill as starting one. If the interview has been effective and the counsellor has entered the other person's life-space, then he must withdraw at the right time and in the right way. With regard to the timing, all managers are busy people and will have set aside a fixed period of time for the counselling session, usually not less than half an hour and not more than one hour. Having a fixed time is important because it puts a creative pressure on both people to get on with things, and enables things to be said at appropriate times. For instance, some things will only be said near the end of an interview, rather than at the beginning. It also means that the counsellor can structure his questions and approach to the time available, so that the end of his counselling work coincides with the end of the time period. When this does not happen, one or both parties leave the interview wishing that they had had more time.

With regard to withdrawal, this should be done in such a way that the client feels satisified with the counselling and is left with a personal piece of work to do. He should not feel complacent, but should feel rather that real help has been received and that something important and useful has been achieved.

SUMMARY

A. If a piece of counselling is to be effective, the counsellor must see his client as he really is, a unique individual, different from anyone else. But differences between people can be the cause of anxiety and fear, and it is easier to categorise people and deal with the label rather than the person. This can result in stereotyping, when, for instance, accountants are all seen as unimaginative introverts or salesmen as hearty extroverts. The counsellor must be aware of these dangers if he is to have a genuine encounter with his client.

B. The concept of 'life-space' helps to ensure that the client is seen as a unique individual. The life-space is the psychological force-field which makes up the private and personal world of each of us. When two people meet in a counselling situation, it is the interaction between these forces which results in their actual behaviour. The concept of life-space can help to illuminate the counselling process.

   1. Entering the life-space: The counsellor cannot force an entrance. He needs an invitation to be allowed in and it requires a climate of trust before the client will voluntarily lower his defences and allow the counsellor to enter his private world.
   2. Behaviour within the life-space: Being allowed into another person's world is a privilege which should not be abused, and within the counselling process criticism is one such abuse. It is not only discourteous, but has the effect of stopping any effective counselling. The client feels threatened and starts to operate his defences.
   3. Exploring the life-space: If the counsellor can help his client explore his own inner world, the client can more effectively examine and analyse what is worrying him. This may involve helping him to recall forgotten facts, look at his problem from a different angle or consider the implications of any intended action.

4. Dealing with emotions and feelings: A person's private world involves feelings and emotions as well as facts and events. Sensitive counselling helps people to get in touch with the feelings associated with their problem and this has a therapeutic effect.

5.Life-space, reality and fantasy: Fantasies are a normal part of everyone's life, helping, as they do, to minimise the harshness of the real world. But counselling can only be effective when the client is enabled to recognise and accept the facts that surround him and to discover realistic solutions.

6. Solutions that fit the life-space: Any new actions or changes which the client decides to make must be congruent with his basic personality and general outlook. Good counselling results in incremental change, rather than quantum jumps.

7. On leaving the life-space: In counselling, the way the meeting concludes is as important as the way in which it commenced. The client should feel that he has received real help and he should carry away with him a personal piece of work to do.

REFERENCES

Lewin, K., 'Need, Force and Valence in Psychological Fields,' in Hollander, E. P. and Hunt, R. G. (eds) *Classic Contributions to Social Psychology, OUP*, London, 1972

7

Developing the Organisation

As soon as people get together and form themselves into an organisation to do some work, a certain 'climate' is created between them. This climate, whilst hard to define precisely, can be felt by a visitor to the organisation and is of course experienced daily by those who work there. Go into any shop in the high street, and from the way you are served and treated, you will get a good idea of the shop's climate. The assistant may be warm and attentive, anxious to help without forcing goods on you. She may bring in one of her colleagues to help and you can judge from the way they work together, that they enjoy working there and that relationships are good. Enter another shop, and you may be met with indifference and a lack of courtesy, and there may be signs of tension among the staff. Clearly, the climate in these two shops is very different.

Every organisation, no matter what size it is, reveals its climate in many ways, some of which are obvious and others more subtle. For instance, the climate might be one in which authority and status are very important, and the ways in which things are organised continually underline this fact. There may be different dining rooms for different classes of people, different size cars symbolising rank, and even different lavatories. A climate in which these differences are continually emphasised must, in some way, affect the efficiency or profitability of the organisation.

Tradition plays a large part in characterising the climate of an organisation. The people who first worked there will have established ways of operating and behaving which suited them. These early methods and procedures become less and less appropriate over the years, but new employees are forced to accept these traditions as the price of membership, although they may be contrary to their own code of values or method of working. If they attempt to change them, they may be branded troublemakers and the organisation can exert a variety of pressures to make them conform.

This holds true for attitudes as well as methods, but attitudes are more difficult to analyse and define. If, for instance, an engineering company is losing orders and its share of the market, it may be relatively easy to recognise that the problem is one of poor product design and old machinery. It would be fairly simple to recommend that the company purchase modern equipment (given that the money was available) and to suggest improvements in the product design.

But the attitudes that exist in an organisation may be equally out-of-date and these have an even greater influence on overall performance. Attitudes of management to shopfloor workers, attitudes towards customers and the marketplace, and especially attitudes of employees to one another are all influenced by the organisation's climate and may reflect past economic or social situations that have long since changed. One important effect of an organisational climate which comprises inappropriate and outdated attitudes is that it fosters all the worst kinds of human feelings and emotions. This is due to the anxiety that is generated when people are forced to work in a climate that at best makes them feel uncomfortable or at worst, frightens and threatens them. Anxiety has a profound effect on behaviour at work, and the various psychological defences which anxious people operate can clearly be seen. In organisations the effects of these are hostility, suspicion, aggression, mistrust and bad relationships.

Successful organisations are those which can adapt to changing circumstances. It is a continuous and evolutionary process, and only those who change effectively survive. Those who fail to change become living fossils and die out. Here is the crux of the problem which faces every organisation in different degrees. On one hand, people in organisations establish patterns of work, attitudes and behaviour which harden into traditions and these are very difficult to change. On the other hand, the very existence of every organisation depends on its ability to develop and adapt itself to meet the constant changes in the environment.

The question that must be asked, therefore, by every manager is, how do you change organisations? There are a huge number of books on the subject and a new semiscience has developed called 'organisational development' which attempts to provide theories of change and to discover practical methods by which organisations can bring it about. Organisational development is still a very imprecise 'science' and perhaps, will necessarily always be so. It has had some success and has confirmed what many managers knew already from their own experience: namely, that attitudes and traditions are extremely difficult to change, especially at work.

An organisation should be able to produce its goods or services efficiently. If it encounters an obstacle, such as increased competition from a rival product or a cheaper service offered by a competitor, it should have the reserves and ability to respond quickly and effectively. A sudden or severe setback may result in a painful process of change involving drastic action, but a healthy organisation will fight back and achieve a full recovery.

To achieve this state of fitness, organisations require efficiency at all levels and a continual awareness of market changes. Few managers would disagree with this statement. The question is whether there is any particular part of an organisation which is vital to this state of health and which can contribute dramatically to the ability to respond quickly and appropriately to change. The answer surely is 'yes': the key area is located in the manager-subordinate relationship. Apart from marriage and the family, the manager-subordinate relationship is the most important relationship in the lives of people at work. Every manager has an effect on the performance of his subordinates and the way in which their work is carried out. Working with a 'good' manager can provide the subordinate with challenging and interesting work with all the range of feelings which result from stimulation and achievement. Such a manager gives appropriate feedback on performance and encouragement for promotion. The 'bad' manager is perceived as unhelpful and critical, perhaps behaving as an autocrat and creating fear and uncertainty.

The relationship a person has with his manager, whether good or bad, is bound to affect his performance and his feelings at work, and quite possibly, his behaviour outside work as well. A manager, similarly, worries about his subordinates and is affected by their behaviour. He may perceive them as good or bad, either eager to work and willing to take on responsibility or else lazy and uncooperative, avoiding work and careless of standards.

Perhaps the biggest effect of this relationship is in the growth and development of the subordinate. An effective manager is aware that the work a subordinate is given to do, together with the way he is treated, will either develop or constrict him. This is made more complex by the fact that the manager is in a position of authority and power over the subordinate. As Elliott Jaques says:

Here is an intensely human situation founded upon a

psychologically and emotionally subtle relationship. It is a social exchange relationship, the outcome of which affects the future success and progress of both the manager and the subordinate. It is not a simple economic exchange relationship. There is a complex underlay of hundreds of unspecified assumptions about appropriate modes of address and speech, giving of praise and criticism, special concessions, time off and special effort. *(A General Theory of Bureaucracy)*

Manager-subordinate relationships are at the heart of any organisation's effectiveness and the better these are, the healthier that organisation will be. After all, in every organisation, there are at least only one less manager-subordinate relationships than there are employees. That is to say, for every 1000 people employed in an organisation, at least 999 are involved in such a relationship. Clearly, the manager-subordinate relationship is very important to the subordinate, the manager and the organisation, and needs more exploration and explanation.

A useful way to proceed is through the idea of counselling: a good manager-subordinate relationship can be defined as a 'counselling relationship'. Counselling means helping, coaching and consulting, and although these activities may have to take place at times specified by the organisation, i.e. counselling at a formal appraisal interview, we are concerned here with an ongoing relationship in which these elements are continually present. There are of course problems in this approach. A good counsellor neither uses nor needs authority in his role, yet by definition a manager has authority over his subordinate. A counsellor helps the person being counselled to form his own solutions. However, a manager has targets, budgets and deadlines which have to be met, and these may have to override his subordinates' plans and his own.

These are real constraints and must be recognised as such, but they do not prevent a manager forming a counselling relationship with his subordinate to their mutual advantage. A clearer description of what this means in

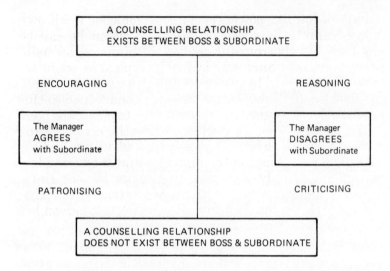

practice can be obtained by considering how a manager who has a counselling relationship with his subordinate behaves (a) when he agrees with his subordinate's action or plans and (b) when he disagrees. This can be compared with a manager in the same situations who does not have a counselling relationship.

The diagram illustrates the four basic behavioural styles a manager may use towards a subordinate, depending on whether a counselling relationship exists or not.

In a non-counselling relationship with his subordinates, the manager will *Patronise* when he agrees and will *Criticise* when he disagrees. But in a counselling relationship, the manager will *Encourage* when he agrees and *Reason* when he disagrees.

Patronising

The patronising manager is one who agrees with his subordinate's action, but does not have a counselling relationship with him. Consequently he is pleased, not so much with what the subordinate is doing, but with the fact that the subordinate is agreeing with him. It confirms his fantasy of god-like powers of creating someone in his own image, essentially a son or daughter whom he can be proud of. The patronising manager thinks in terms of rewards or punishments and when he is pleased, wishes to show this approval by giving some extra cash, or time off. Either way, the subordinate becomes conditioned to this kind of behaviour and tries increasingly to please the boss. And it becomes clear that what pleases the boss is acting more and more like him. The result is a subordinate who is not only a pale image of the manager, but is less and less himself and heavily dependent on his boss. His one aim is to please and, like a dog, he learns all the tricks that bring a reward. He learns not how to be an effective person but how to get the boss to open the biscuit tin.

Criticising

The criticising manager is one who disagrees with his subordinate's action and does not have a counselling relationship with him. He is essentially angry either openly or in a cold, controlled manner, because his own ideas of what is right or wrong have been challenged. Consequently the subordinate must be made to feel guilty and to experience his heavy displeasure in order to apologise and repent of his misdeeds. The critical manager will punish where he can, but where he has no open means of punishment, he will use his anger or else withdraw his friendship and affection. The re-establishment of relationships is a sign that the subordinate has been forgiven but also serves as a warning of what will happen if he errs again in the future. The result is a subordinate who spends a great deal of his time ensuring that his work and behaviour are in line with his boss's expectations and this can also involve his attitudes and opinions about the world in general. The dependence that this creates stifles initiative and encourages conformity and an over-regard for rules, regulations and procedures.

Reasoning

The reasoning manager is one who disagrees with his
subordinate's plans or performance and has a counselling
relationship with him. Instead of criticising, he explains
the reasons for his disagreement and through direct questioning, helps the subordinate to face up to the facts of the
situation and explore the likely consequences of his proposed action. The reasoning manager also has the humility
to recognise that he is not the sole repository of truth and
that a manager is not endowed with infallibility. Consequently, as he reasons with his subordinate he himself is
open to the influence of fact and reason and may change
his own mind, or modify his views. But if, at the end of it
all, both remain unconvinced and the subordinate is still
intent on a course of action with which the manager disagrees, the reasoning manager will take one of two courses of
action. He may allow the subordinate to carry on, cal-
culating that the risk involved is outweighed by the learning the subordinate may achieve by making a mistake.
Or he may say 'no', repeat his reasons and exercise his
legitimate authority. His right to do this stems from the
fact that, in the last analysis, he is held accountable for his
subordinate's performance. The outcome of this kind of
behaviour is enormously valuable for the subordinate. He
learns to evaluate his decisions and analyse the consequences of his actions. He learns how to use reason to state
his case and argue his point. He learns to listen to another,
and different, point of view and to modify and change his
outlook without suffering a 'loss of face'. Most importantly, he learns from his manager how he might exercise
his own authority in the future if he gets promotion. He is
encouraged to be himself, to use to the full his own unique
ideas and skills and at the same time, to recognise the
genuine authority of his boss, without being frightened or
unduly influenced by it. Finally, he also learns to recognise those issues which for him are vital, and where he
must stand firm, even insisting on seeing a higher
authority.

Encouraging

The encouraging manager is one who basically agrees
with his subordinate's actions and who has a counselling
relationship with him. He gives praise and congratula-
tions and helps the subordinate to gain the maximum
recognition for his successes. Although he ensures that
there are the proper financial rewards for such efforts, he
is equally concerned to see that his subordinate has
further opportunities for future achievement. He tries to
increase the subordinate's personal and professional
development through increasingly challenging work, and
balances new responsibilities with appropriate coaching
and training. He shows his trust by delegating more of his
own work to the subordinate and by involving him in
increased consultation and decision-making. Finally, if he
feels that the subordinate has outgrown his present job, he
strongly recommends his promotion even though he will
lose him. However, he believes that there are plenty of
other good people around and he would like the chance to
develop their potential. It is also likely that the
encouraging manager will get promotion himself,
because, of course, he now has a very suitable replace-
ment.

CONCLUSION

Whilst formal counselling may take place at specified
times during a year, its effectiveness depends on the quality of the relationship which exists the year round. The
manager who is an effective counsellor has an attitude
towards his subordinates which develops trust and openness between them at all times. The aim of the manager
should be to build up a relationship which is not dominated by his greater authority, but is based on the essential characteristics of good human relationships. This is
not to deny the real differences between a boss and his

subordinate; it is to concentrate on the interdependence of the two roles and maximise co-operation and mutual assistance.

The strength of the boss-subordinate relationship is crucial to the effectiveness of the organisation, and directly affects its ability to change in response to new demands and situations.

SUMMARY

A. Every organisation develops a climate within it which consists of the unwritten rules which govern the ways in which people are expected to behave. This climate has a profound influence on everyone's behaviour and its acceptance is the price each person pays for his continuing membership.

B. An inappropriate climate, consisting of outmoded attitudes and traditions, can be as detrimental to an organisation's effectiveness as out-of-date plant and equipment. Every organisation must be able to adapt to meet changes in the environment if it is to be successful, but it is harder to change attitudes than machinery. The problem facing managers is how to maintain a stable organisation which at the same time has the flexibility to respond quickly to new circumstances.

C. The key to organisational flexibility lies in the manager-subordinate relationship. This relationship is at the heart of the organisation and has an effect on employees at every level, influencing not only their work performance but also their general morale.

D. An effective relationship between a boss and his subordinate can be characterised as a counselling relationship. This is demonstrated by the way they work together day by day, and it also enables the boss to counsel his subordinate when this is appropriate.

E. There are four basic behavioural styles which a manager may adopt towards his subordinate. These styles become apparent specifically when the manager agrees or disagrees with his subordinate. If there is not a counselling relationshp between them, the manager will Patronise when he agrees and Criticise when he disagrees. But in a counselling relationship he will Encourage when he agrees and Reason when he disagrees.

Patronising — The patronising manager behaves essentially as a father, proud that his child is following in his
footsteps and agreeing with his own suggestions. As a
result the subordinate tries more and more to please
him and is in danger of becoming a 'yes-man'.

Criticising — The criticising manager becomes angry
when he disagrees with his subordinate and will try to
punish him. This creates fear and dependency in the
subordinate who will then stick closely to rules and
precedence in order to avoid any future penalties.

Reasoning — The reasoning manager explains why he
disagrees but allows his subordinate to explain his point
of view and argue his case. He is prepared to change his
mind as a result of the discussion, but in the last
analysis he is accountable for his subordinate's work
and reserves the right to say 'no'.

Encouraging — The encouraging manager is pleased
with his subordinate's performance and makes sure
that he receives due recognition. Through delegation
and appropriate training he encourages him to undertake greater responsibility and develop his own unique
talents.

8

Anxiety and Stress At Work

Anybody who has ever tried to counsel, whether formally or informally, will have experienced anxiety – that sense of foreboding, the unpleasant feeling in the pit of the stomach, the fear that something unexpected will happen which will have an unpleasant effect.

In order to counsel effectively, it is essential for the counsellor to understand the nature of anxiety. Firstly, he must be able to recognise it in the person he is trying to help and this will enable him to understand that person's behaviour more clearly. Secondly, and perhaps more importantly, he must be able to recognise his own anxiety and the reasons for it, and be able to cope with it. Perhaps the most important characteristic of the effective counsellor is that he is able to contain his own anxiety. The most disastrous effect of anxiety on counselling is that it makes the counsellor want to do something, and takes him, from being client-centred, to being problem-centred. In these cases, the motive for his activity is not the well-being of the person being counselled, but the relief of his own anxiety. In many cases, simply to sit and listen without doing anything is extremely difficult and the more anxious one feels, the more difficult this becomes. But an understanding of the nature of anxiety and the ability to contain it are the hallmark of a mature counsellor and the prerequisite of helping.

THE NATURE OF ANXIETY

Anxiety is an intensely personal and subjective feeling. What is a challenge to one man may result in a nervous breakdown in another. Because anxiety is so basic and common, it can be too easily dismissed as merely part of the human condition. In fact, there are some managers who deliberately create anxiety in their departments. 'Keeps them on their toes. They never know where I'll hit them next.' This tendency can be seen especially in interviewing; some managers like to put interviewees under stress, to see how they cope. The results of such interviews are probably worthless.

But what causes this anxiety that is common to everybody and to all organisations? And what are its effects? And why should anxiety be singled out from the wide spectrum of human emotions as worthy of special consideration? One answer lies in the acute forms that anxiety can take. Most people will admit that some of their most unpleasant times have been when they have experienced acute anxiety. At a less intense level, a phone call from the boss's secretary saying that he wants to see you can create anxiety. The big conference where you have to make a speech can be terrifying; so, too, can the situation in which you have to tell some of your staff that they are redundant. These are specific experiences but you may also feel anxious for a whole variety of reasons that can be very difficult to analyse, yet result in a general feeling of unease and stress, which you carry around and which is extremely hard to overcome and dissipate. Anxiety always creates the same symptoms whether the cause is real or imaginery. The palms sweat, the heart pounds, blood pressure increases and the bowels may be affected. If anxiety is experienced as stress over a long period, then a whole range of seemingly physical ills may result, ranging from headaches and bad backs to high blood pressure, ulcers and heart attacks. The explanation for these physical responses to anxiety probably lies in the pre-history of man. When primitive man was faced by a savage animal or a hostile tribesman, he had only two courses of action open to him for survival – fight or flight. To carry out either of these strategies successfully required increased strength and energy. The heart needed to beat faster to carry oxygen to the muscles. Muscles were tensed, ready for quick action. The bowels emptied to lose weight, and adrenalin was pumped into the bloodstream ready to help clotting if the person was wounded. The more this happened, the more likely our primitive ancestors were to emerge successfully from fighting and overcoming the enemy or running away from the threat. We respond to danger in exactly the same way as our ancestors did half a million years ago. Anxiety is man's response to danger. This danger may be real or imaginery, but if he feels threatened, for whatever reason, he will experience some or all of the physical responses mentioned. If the danger is obvious and immediate, he can still react in the old primitive way. For instance, if attacked by a young thug on the way home, a man will automatically respond to this danger by fighting to overcome the attacker, or by running away as fast as possible. People often describe how, in these circumstances, they find a new strength and energy which they didn't know they possessed. In fact, they used the physical responses which anxiety automatically brings out to overcome danger. But in modern society, and especially in complex organisations, many anxieties are caused by much more diffuse and imprecise dangers than

actual physical attacks, and the response of fight or flight
is impossible or inappropriate.

A manager in a large engineering group provides a good
illustration. A design engineer by training, he gradually
got promoted until he was made responsible for the new
computer systems department. But he knew little about
the use of computers and felt increasingly threatened by
the bright young graduates who were being recruited as
systems analysts. He couldn't express these fears either to
his colleagues, whom he imagined would accuse him of
incompetence, or to himself. Feeling threatened, he
became increasingly anxious and started to sleep badly
and have severe headaches. Eventually, he went to his
doctor, frightened that he had some dreaded disease, like
cancer or a brain tumour. Luckily he had a patient and
discerning GP, who helped the engineer to realise that the
origin of his illness was the anxiety he was experiencing
in his job. This example also helps to illustrate the nature
of acute stress. Acute stress is simply prolonged anxiety.
The bodily symptoms of anxiety originally evolved to
assist immediate survival action in a dangerous situation.
But if the dangerous situation continues over a long time
and cannot be resolved through fight or flight, the body
responds in the same way. Adrenalin will be continually
injected into the bloodstream, resulting in high pulse
rates and possible clotting and embolisms. Muscles continually tensed result in headaches and backaches. Blood
pressure may remain high, and all sorts of bowel and
stomach disorders may occur. Sexual potency may well be
affected, because a person feeling endangered is unlikely
to give much thought to sexual pleasure and procreation.

Problems which cause anxiety at work can be overcome
and mastered, provided they can be described and shared.
In other words, reality must be faced up to. Increasing
market share, developing new products, or improving a
company's cash flow position – problems of this sort are
part of the very nature of managing, and should not cause
acute anxiety.

But acute anxiety can arise from the areas of interpersonal relations and self-esteem, which are difficult to

describe and even more difficult to share. It can be very hard for a manager to face up to the reality that his job is too much for him; even harder, perhaps, to do something about it; harder, also, to resolve a situation where the boss appears autocratic and bullying. Even if the logical decision is flight – i.e. leave the organisation – economic and family pressures may make this impossible. Managers locked into large organisations are particularly vulnerable to feelings of anxiety, which, if unresolved, can develop into stress, with all its attendant ills and miseries.

So far, anxiety has been discussed in the context of some danger external to the individual, such as an attack by a thug, or working under an autocratic boss. In other words, situations in which there is real objective danger; the bad feeling which this causes is called 'objective anxiety'. But what about those occasions when people feel anxious for no obvious reason, that is when no objective fact seems to account for it? Everyone has memories and past experiences, fears and worries which are locked inside themselves and to which they do not wish to admit. These are all capable of creating anxiety, and if nothing is done about them, they can produce the unpleasant symptoms already described. Because these thoughts and fears arise from within, the feeling they produce is called 'neurotic anxiety'. So far as the individual is concerned, the anxieties are equally real. The most obvious defence against neurotic anxiety is called repression. Repression means burying the memory or fear as deeply as possible under the level of the conscious mind. There the anxious person hopes it will stay, out of sight and (apparently) out of mind. But, of course, it remains somewhere inside his head and will probably trouble him at some future date. Or it may sneak into his dreams.

Another personal defence mechanism is called projection. This is a subtle process. The mind tricks itself into believing that the cause of the anxiety is located in somebody else. For instance, a manager who has had a poor education may feel deeply envious and threatened by the young graduates entering the company whom he sees as cleverer and more able than himself. By using the process

of projection, the manager gets rid of his anxiety, changing 'I am envious of you' into 'You are envious of me'. He
can now begin to treat the graduates harshly, convinced
that these new boys want his job and are not prepared to do
a hard day's work.

'Forget all about that fancy college stuff. You won't
learn anything until you've got your hands dirty. I didn't
get where I am today by book-learning.' The source of his
anxiety is now (apparently) external and objective, and so
he can fight it. Small wonder if after 18 months the graduate leaves, fed up with boring jobs and being treated like
an idiot. This, of course, only confirms the manager in his
beliefs. 'There you are. They think the world owes them a
living. Not like it was in my day.' The real source of the
manager's anxiety, his feelings of being poorly educated,
remains with him, and unless it is dealt with, he is likely
to behave in exactly the same way to the next graduate.

Another example of projection is the person at work who
feels attracted to someone of his or her own sex. Such
feelings (perhaps more common than people care to admit)
may cause great anxiety. By using projection, the feeling
'I have homosexual feelings towards you' is transformed
into 'You have homosexual feelings towards me'. Again,
the source is now externalised, and so the person can
attack the other verbally or even physically, and show his
hatred of this disgusting behaviour. The real source of the
anxiety remains. It has been said that projection is the
basis for all moral indignation.

How does anxiety within people relate to that within
organisations? A whole range of outside factors can
threaten the organisation's survival, such as getting a
better market share, recruiting a good labour force,
increasing sales. All of these things can be tackled by
'fight or flight' behaviour. The sales director at the annual
conference says 'We're going to beat hell out of the opposition'. Competition in business can even be seen as stylised
warfare, played within certain rules, where there are
winners and losers.

But what of the feelings of anxiety which arise for
reasons within the organisation, like the neurotic anxiety

which arises from within the individual? An individual defends himself from these unpleasant feelings by such methods as repression and projection. What does an organisation do? There are three possible ways in which an organisation (or part of it, such as a department) can behave in an attempt to deal with internal problems which are causing intense anxiety and which it is unwilling or unable to face.

The first is *dependency:* people put their complete trust and hope in the leader. There is a general assumption that he, and he alone, will deliver the organisation out of all its problems without the need for any effort by others. Everyone else feels powerless and waits for the leader to achieve results as if by magic. Examples of the dependency mode of behaviour are legion, especially in politics. The members of a particular party place all their hopes in one person, believing against all experience and reason that this president or prime minister will usher in the golden age.

In industry and commerce, the same process occurs. The organisation faced with internal problems and difficulties appoints a new man and everyone waits to see what he will do. But what can the leader do? The internal problems can never be resolved simply by waiting for the leader to come up with the answer. In organisational terms, the problems which are causing the anxiety can only be resolved when they can be described and shared. This means hard work and analysis by everyone and involves the opposite of dependency – co-operation and mutual trust. If the leader can lead the organisation to work in this productive way, then the anxieties will diminish. But if the leader colludes in this fantasy that he alone can do it, then both he and the organisation are heading for trouble. Not only will he ignore the talents and abilities of his people, but he must inevitably fail in the role which he has accepted. The whole of history is littered with failed leaders who accepted this dependency role, and sooner or later failed to live up to the impossible expectations of their followers. Few dictators die peacefully; at a lower level, many whiz-kids brought in to save ailing companies last only a very short time. The solution to internal problems in organisations needs the application and co-operation of all the members if the problems are to be confronted and resolved. The 'dependency' leader may initially make people feel all is well, but ultimately he will fail – and the odium of failure will tarnish his reputation.

The second, related way in which an organisation may behave to protect itself against internal anxiety is *messianic hope.'* A general assumption is made that soon somebody or something will appear on the scene to deliver everybody from all their troubles. 'Our economic problems will be solved when North Sea oil comes on stream.' 'Once we have the computer installed, we shall have no more problems with invoicing customers.' Perhaps this particular defence against anxiety is seen best in the way some firms use training departments or external consultants to teach the 'latest thing'. Companies are full of the decaying skeletons of management by objective schemes, which were once believed to be the answer to low motivation and achievement. T-groups, once thought to offer incomparable improvement in interpersonal relations, are now viewed with the deepest suspicion. Blake and Moulton's managerial grid with its scales leading up to maximum concern for production on one axis and maximum concern for people on the other is beginning to sound distinctly old-fashioned.

This is not to be cynical about training. But managers should distrust trainers and consultants who have the answer at a price of £100 per head. Such false hopes will always lead to cynicism and failure, because the anxieties which arise from within the organisation are untouched by these cosmetics. One very large company, which had innumerable internal problems concerning both production and relationships, spent hundreds of hours and thousands of pounds employing specialists to work on a graduate recruitment scheme. The hope was that all problems would be solved by introducing bright young people into every part of the company. It is doubtful if one per cent have remained with that firm, which is now on the verge of collapse. What was needed at that time was a concentrated effort to straighten out production, regularise supplies and improve the awful labour relations. The company, which could not face up to these anxiety-creating problems, misplaced its hopes on graduate recruitment.

The third defence which an organisation may adopt towards its internal anxiety is that of *fight or flight* behaviour. Parts of the organisation fight against each other, convinced that they are being 'got at' by head office or that there must be a 'show-down' with the unions. This fighting is essentially paranoic and inevitably results in a depletion of energy.

Such behaviour throws up the worst sort of leader – one who is convinced he is waging a holy war. Attacks are entirely misdirected. Attacking head office through all the manoeuvres known to management will not resolve the root problems which are causing the anxieties. Again, the only way forward is through the hard work and co-operation of people in the organisation in an attempt to face up to the real problems.

Anxiety is one of the main causes of inefficiency, both in people and organisations. Because it is such an unpleasant feeling they are bound to develop ways of protecting themselves from anxiety. In itself, protection can lead to effective ways of behaviour: our ancestors survived the various dangers they faced, through fight or flight behaviour. But the causes of anxiety that come from within the person or the organisation can lead to behaviour that is both ineffective and wasteful of energy. The more the individual resorts to repression and projection, the less energy he has with which to face reality and live a normal and healthy life.

This is also true of organisations. The three modes of behaviour described – dependency, 'messianic' hope and fight/flight – all absorb energy. The more the organisation behaves in these ways, the less energy there is available to deal with the realities of cash flow, the changing market and the proper aspirations of its employees. It will always reveal hostility, rivalry and suspicion, and its social life, as well as its business efficiency, will run down. On the other hand, the more an organisation can minimise anxiety by helping its people to be in touch with what is really happening, both around them and within them, the more each individual is able to direct his mental energy towards his work and the aims of the company. Organisations which operate in this way are characterised by co-operation, and a climate which encourages the formation of relationships based on mutual trust and respect. Such a company, able to face up to the problems of its internal anxieties, will develop as an open system, able to regenerate itself and react appropriately to the constantly changing environment. Clearly, counselling can make a vital contribution to this process, enabling people to deal effectively with their problems and enabling the organisation to achieve its corporate goals.

SUMMARY

A. Anxiety is one of the most common unpleasant feelings which people experience. It is a reaction to a perceived threat and triggers off a number of physiological responses which enable a person to take effective action by overcoming or escaping from the danger. If anxiety is prolonged, it produces stress. When the automatic physiological responses cannot be channeled into effective fight or flight behaviour, they begin to damage the body, resulting in such symptoms as high blood pressure, headaches, backaches and stomach and bowel disorders.

B. Anxiety caused by a real threat, such as a physical attack, is called 'objective anxiety' and is reduced when the source of the threat is overcome or avoided. But what of the anxieties which arise from within the person himself, due possibly to past fears and memories? This is called 'neurotic anxiety' and is more difficult to deal with. People develop a number of psychological defences to cope with it, such as repression and projection, but neither deal effectively with the problem. Both objective and neurotic anxiety cause the same bodily reactions and in either case anxiety is reduced only when the root cause of the threat is faced and moved.

C. Anxiety affects organisations as well as individuals. The objective source of anxiety may come from increased competition or a reduction in sales and this causes the same fight/flight reactions. When this happens the organisation tries to overcome the opposition or take evasive action, through effective corporate strategies.

D. But what of the internal factors within the organisation which can give rise to anxiety, in the same way that an individual experiences neurotic anxiety? In this case, the interplay of the emotions and feelings of many people results in specific patterns of organisational behaviour which are essentially corporate defences against anxiety.

Three of these defences can be identified:

Dependency — In this mode of behaviour everyone puts their trust in a leader and there is the general assumption that he, unaided, will deliver them from all their troubles and problems. Everyone feels powerless and there is a belief that the leader has limitless and almost magical powers.

'Messianic' hope — In this instance, there is a general assumption that some person or event will soon appear on the scene which will solve all the organisation's problems, such as North Sea oil, a new computer installation or the latest training package.

Fight or flight — This is not the legitimate fight against competition but the fighting which occurs within the organisation, such as fighting between the production department and the sales office or between management and the unions.

E. These three modes of behaviour help people avoid coming to terms with the real issues within the organisation which are making them anxious. They drain productive energy away from the proper corporate objectives and reduce efficiency. It is only when there is a climate of trust and openness that everyone can communicate and share their concerns and deal with the reality of organisational life. Counselling, and the counselling relationship, can make a significant contribution to this aim.

9

A Checklist For Counsellors

So far, this book has looked at different aspects of counselling in order to illustrate some of the processes which occur when counselling takes place. But counselling is essentially a practical piece of work where theories and ideas have to show themselves in effective performance. The following is a checklist which should help managers to carry out a good counselling interview.

1. What is the purpose of the interview?

Whenever possible, the manager should find time to consider the purpose of the interview. Of course this cannot happen when the meeting develops from some sort of crisis which finds a subordinate in distress. The reasons for the

counselling interview may include all or some of the following:

(a) To help the interviewee let off steam;
(b) To help him to see himself or his problem more
clearly;
(c) To support him while he finds his own solutions and
makes his own decisions;
(d) To demonstrate interest and genuine concern.

It is a useful exercise to write down the following two
statements: 'As a result of this interview, I hope that I will
. . .' and 'As a result of this interview, I hope that he will
. . .'.

2. What information do I need?

It has been known for a manager to commence his interview by saying 'Good morning Keith' only to hear the
response 'Actually I'm Peter!' The manager must have as
much information as possible concerning the person he is
going to counsel. If it is an interview concerning performance appraisal, then he will want to know what happened at the previous interview and the significant
achievements and failures of the subordinate's subsequent performance. The manager should take time to
assimilate all the information and it is a good idea to make
brief notes on a small piece of paper which can easily be
referred to during the interview. It can be quite unnerving
to the subordinate if the manager is continually bur-
rowing into a file – the message comes over very clearly, 'I
don't know much about you'.

3. Have I ensured privacy?

There are few things more counter-productive to a counselling interview than interruptions of any kind. The
telephone must not be allowed to ring. If the manager is
connected to his secretary's phone, then he can easily ask

her not to put through any calls. Otherwise, the phone should be taken off the hook. People must be prevented from coming into the office by fixing a notice on the door saying 'meeting in progress'. Managers who do not have a room to themselves or else work in an office that is open-planned, must negotiate for a private room in which to hold the interview.

4. Where shall we sit?

There is no doubt that the physical arrangement of the room has a strong influence on the way in which a counselling interview proceeds. Most managers do their work sitting behind a desk and automatically take up that position when counselling a subordinate. But a desk may be much more than simply a useful piece of furniture for writing. It can also be a symbol of authority, which clearly indicates that he who sits behind it is more important than he who sits in front of it. It can also be a barrier, defining boundaries of privacy which must not be crossed. Counselling is likely to be more effective when both people sit facing each other on chairs of the same height without a desk between them, although a low coffee table may be useful for papers.

5. What time shall I need for the interview?

The first aspect of planning is time. When will you hold the interview? Have you allowed at least ten minutes before it so that you are relaxed and have time to refresh your memory of the facts? And, perhaps more importantly, how long have you allowed for the interview itself? This will of course depend on how busy you are and the importance you give to the subject under discussion. But it is unlikely that less than half an hour will be sufficient and probably not more than an hour will be needed. Having decided on the length of the interview, it is important that the manager informs the subordinate of this at the outset. Finally, have you allowed at least quarter of an hour between the end of the interview and your next engagement? This time is needed to reflect on what has happened and to make any notes. It also ensures that the manager does not spend the last ten minutes of the interview looking at his watch and mentally preparing for the next appointment.

6. What is the best plan for the interview?

A counselling interview needs to be properly managed if it is going to be useful, and it requires appropriate direction by the manager. This can only happen if the counsellor prepares an outline plan which makes full use of the time available. One basic approach is 'WASP' where W = welcome, A = acquiring information, S = supplying information, P = parting. Skilful planning of the interview ensures that the counselling process is completed within the allotted time.

7. How shall I start the interview?

Interviews have been described as 'a conversation with a purpose'. When a conversation begins, it is usual for the people involved to talk about such seemingly irrelevant matters as the weather, sport or the state of each other's health. But these opening gambits have a real purpose – they set the scene and establish an initial rapport which facilitates the discussion of more important matters to follow. The same is true in commencing an interview. The manager must welcome his subordinate and set the scene in which an appropriate counselling interview can ensue. The more the subordinate can feel relaxed and at ease, the more he will speak openly and frankly about his attitudes and feelings. Getting down to business too soon can result in the subordinate feeling tense and apprehensive.

8. What kind of relationship do I want to establish?

The relationship established in a counselling interview is
bound to reflect the day-to-day relationship which already
exists between the manager and his subordinate. If the
normal relationship is slightly cold and remote, then the
manager will have to work very hard to establish a
warmer and more friendly atmosphere. On the other
hand, too much *bonhomie* from the manager, especially if
this is unusal, may worry the subordinate and make him
wonder if he is being softened up before hearing the bad
news. The best relationship is one in which both parties
feel at ease and can behave naturally and feel able to
speak openly and honestly. It should also be such that it
contributes to the future working relationship.

9. What information needs to be exchanged?

Counselling depends on getting down to the facts,
although initially what may be fact to one may not seem
true to the other. If you are counselling on performance,
then you must have as much fact as possible about what
your subordinate has achieved and the way he has gone
about his work. If there are failures you should be
especially sure of your facts and be able to present these to
the subordinate in a non-threatening way. After all, the
aim of counselling is to find ways of overcoming problems
such as poor performance, and not to play the role of
sentencing judge. Part of the information you may have to
convey may be bad news, such as failure to achieve a pay
rise or a promotion. The important thing here is to give the
reasons and also to take responsibility for your decision. A
subordinate can feel very nonplussed if he is told that
'they' have refused an application for promotion. But if he
is told that you have made this decision and for the following reasons, then he can discuss it with you (he may
even get angry) and discover what he should do to improve
his chances in the future. Or, and this may be the most
difficult, he may realise that he has no future chances for

promotion, and counselling can help him to come to grips with this reality.

10. What kind of questions should I ask?

Invariably in counselling, the open-ended question is the best kind to ask. An open-ended question is one which allows the client the maximum choice in his reply and enables him to explore his own reactions to the full. Such questions could be:

'Would you like to tell me more about that?'
'Why do you say that?'
'What did you do then?'
'What are you going to do now?'
'If you go ahead and do that, what do you think will be the consequence?'

The opposite type of questioning produces from the subordinate 'yes' or 'no' answers.

11. How can I help him explore his feelings?

In any counselling interview the manager must encourage his subordinate to express his feelings. By his behaviour and the nature of their relationship, he must indicate that this is perfectly legitimate and acceptable. The manager must be prepared to experience his subordinate's emotions, such as sadness or anger, and his own emotions. A counselling interview without the expression and experience of feelings can never be fully effective. The classic question to ask is simply 'How did that make you feel?' or to deal with the immediate situation, 'How are you feeling now?'. Dealing with feelings is especially important when people come to you with a personal problem and request an interview; the effective counsellor knows that on these occasions, emotions and feelings are always part of the problem. Their expression is frequently therapeutic and contributes directly to resolving the particular problem.

12. How can I ensure that appropriate action will be taken?

An effective counselling interview will frequently end with one or both parties agreeing to take some particular action. For the subordinate, this may be something very practical, and the manager should make certain that they both agree on this and understand how it will be achieved. The subordinate may agree to do something less tangible, involving changes in attitude or personal behaviour. The manager also frequently agrees to take some action. But he must be careful. Good counselling can often be exhilarating for both people concerned, with a real sense of achievement and the pleasure of human relationship. The manager must be careful not to promise what he cannot fulfil or what is outside of his authority or company policy. In the 'supplying information' stage, he may need to state clearly company policy so that any action which is taken is within the boundaries of his authority and overall company policy.

13. How shall I conclude the interview?

The way in which an interview is concluded is as important as the way it commences. Those last words spoken, the warmth of the final handshake, all leave a flavour which will remain as significant memories in the subordinate's mind. Careful management of time is important so that completion of counselling work coincides with the end of the allocated time period. The last five minutes are best used for a recapitulation of what has been agreed and especially what action both parties have agreed to take. It also provides an opportunity to ensure that the relationship is sound, especially if strong words have been exchanged during the interview. The aim is for both parties to come from the interview feeling that problems have been resolved and that mutual understanding has been increased.

SUMMARY

1 Determining the purpose of the interview:
   What do you want to achieve?
2 Preparation for the interview:
   Have you got all the information you need concerning
   your subordinate?
3 Ensuring privacy:
   Have you made certain that you will not be interrupted?
4 Seating arrangements:
   Are the chairs in the best position?
5 Planning the time:
   Have you allowed enough time before your next
   appointment?
6 Planning the structure of the interview:
   Have you made an outline plan for the interview?
7 Starting the interview:
   How will you begin so that you will set the client at
   ease?
8 Establishing a counselling relationship:
   How friendly do you want to be?
9 Exchanging information:
   Have you got all the facts and information you may
   need to give?
10 Asking the appropriate questions:
   Have you considered some open-ended questions you
   might ask?
11 Exploration of feelings:
   Are you prepared to allow him to express his feelings?
12 Concluding the interview:
   Have you thought about how you will finish the
   interview?
13 Taking appropriate action:
   Are you prepared to follow up the interview with
   appropriate action?

Appendix I: Training For Counselling

For many people, counselling can be a frightening thing to contemplate doing, simply because they have never received any training for it. At work, counselling skills are one of a number which managers are supposed to 'pick up' as they climb the ladder of promotion. Fortunately, many people are realising that management is a collection of knowledge and skills which can be studied and learnt but there are still too many organisations where technical skills are taken as signs of management potential and that it is the best technicians who are promoted. Of course, common sense, intelligence and the ability to learn from experience can help people to become good managers. But the ability to counsel effectively is unlikely to be acquired in this way. Since counselling can make a powerful contribution to developing both personal and organisational effectiveness, then training in counselling skills is vital to anyone who is responsible for the work of others.

For the past ten years I have been involved in helping managers develop their counselling skills and I have developed a training method which is effective. It is certainly not original, but it is simple and I pass it on in the hope that others may benefit from it.

GENERAL SITUATION

The ideal method requires one tutor to each group of three trainee counsellors. The tutors should be people who have a good understanding of counselling from both a practical and a theoretical standpoint and who are also good teachers – a combination not always easy to find! The total number of people who could attend such a programme clearly depends on the number of competent tutors available, but where possible, I like to work with a group of 12 trainees – and we therefore require a total of four tutors.

A room is needed big enough to allow all the tutors and trainees to sit down comfortably together and where there is a flipboard or blackboard. There also needs to be room for each group to work separately in total privacy. On residential courses, bedrooms are often used for this purpose.

STARTING THE PROGRAMME

The purpose of the day

The tutor who is directing the training should welcome the trainees and, after making any necessary administrative points, state very clearly the purpose of the day. I find it remarkable that people can organise training courses without being certain what their teaching objectives are. I find it even more remarkable that people attend courses equally uncertain why they are there or what their own learning objectives are. Anyone organising counselling training must make sure that in any written material sent out before the course the purpose of that course is stated clearly and unambiguously. This must also be spelt out at the start of the day and written up so that it is clearly seen by everyone.

I use the term 'primary task' and the following form of words: 'The primary task of this training day is to provide members with the opportunity to understand, learn and practise the skills which are necessary for effective counselling.' I then say, half-jokingly, that if anyone does not want to do this, then now is the time to leave. So far, no one has walked out, but it does make the point that we now have a contract between us, and as we shall see later, this enables tutors and trainees to play their proper roles.

The tutor's role

The directing tutor will then outline the programme, pointing out that later on the trainees will be working in trios, each trio having its own tutor. At this stage he will introduce the tutors and briefly describe their role. Their role, when working with the trios is that of consultant, which is a variant of counsellor. They are there, not to teach or instruct, but to act as catalysts in the learning situation. In essence, their role is to maximise the learning for each individual. (It goes without saying that all the tutors will have met beforehand and discussed and agreed their role.)

The 'ice-breaker' exercise

Counselling training requires a climate of trust and openness if it is to be effective. Anyone coming on a training day – especially one dealing with interpersonal skills – is likely to feel anxious and apprehensive at the start. What are the other people like? Are they friendly? Will I make a fool of myself? Will it be worth the time involved? If I was sent on this course, does it mean I have poor social skills? All these questions are likely to be in the minds of the trainees and it is essential that these fears and worries are reduced before any proper training begins. For this reason, I start with an 'ice-breaking' exercise, which is commonly used on a variety of training courses.

The trainees are invited to pair up with someone they don't know (or with the person they know least well), find a quiet corner somewhere and then interview each other with the purpose of finding out as much as they can about one another. I always invite them to try to discover information not only about each other's job and interests, but also why they have come on this training day and what they hope to get out of it. The interviews last a quarter of an hour each, so that this exercise lasts for half an hour. It is usually very effective. The trainees becomes transformed from a quiet and apprehensive group of strangers into a number of pairs who are talking animatedly to each other.

After this half hour, the trainees resume their original seats and then each is given two minutes to introduce the person they have been interviewing to the rest of the group. Of course, people start to ask questions and slowly the anxiety begins to disappear as they realise that the others are not so different from themselves and that they share many common problems and interests.

THE LECTURE

Following the 'ice-breaker' exercise, a tutor gives a lecture of about 30 minutes, in which he outlines the purpose and method of counselling. It is essential that the trainees understand the theory of counselling: I am a great believer in the dictum of Kurt Lewin 'There's nothing so practical as a good theory!' Every tutor will have his own approach and will want to emphasise those points which he thinks are particularly important. If the tutor can make four strong points in his 30-minute lecture, he will be doing well. As an example, here are the headings from the lecture I give; in practice, of course, I vary this a great deal, depending on my audience and how I am feeling at the time.

Outline Lecture Notes

1. The purpose of counselling —
        to help a person examine and solve his own problems
2. What hinders counselling? —
        closed questions
        too much talking by the counsellor
        giving advice
        criticism.
3. What helps counselling? —
        active listening
        open and reflective questions
        a relationship of trust and openness
        the recognition of the person as being important.
4. The value of counselling —
        it reduces anxiety and worry
        it increases personal growth and development
        it increases the effectiveness of the subordinate
        it increases the effectiveness of the department and
        the organisation.

I then allow half an hour for questions and discussion, in which all of the tutors take part.

THE COUNSELLING EXERCISE IN TRIOS

Selecting a real problem

There can be little doubt that the more realistic the training situation can be made, the more learning will be acquired. It is for this reason that I invite trainees in counselling to bring with them a real problem that is currently concerning and worrying them and about which they would like some help. There is of course no way in which anyone can be forced to reveal a problem which they would otherwise have kept hidden, but one can certainly encourage people to be brave and bold. I also say that, as far as possible, the problem should be work related. Initially some people are taken aback and are clearly concerned by this request. Those who find this idea too threatening are told that they can make up a problem or bring one that they used to have. But I also point out that past or imaginery problems can never have the emotional content which a real, current problem generates, and, to that extent, it will not be a good training vehicle. I add that whilst the aim of the exercise is to give people an opportunity to practise their counselling skills, there is a bonus in that the person presenting the problem is very likely to receive real help.

Briefing for the counselling exercise

The directing tutor now describes the procedure for carrying out the counselling exercise in the trios:

Each exercise commences with a counselling interview in which Mr A is the counsellor, Mr B is the client and Mr C is the observer. The tutor plays the role of consultant. This interview should last for approximately 15 minutes, during which time the observer remains perfectly quiet and unobtrusive. The next stage is for the observer to recount what he has seen and to evaluate the performance of the counsellor. The counsellor and client may well wish to join in the debate and the aim should be for Mr A to learn as much as he can about how well he performed and to see where and how he might make improvements. At the same time, the other two will also be learning and considering what this means for them. The evaluation and learning stage is crucial, and could last up to half an hour. The process of interview and evaluation is then repeated twice so that each member of the group has played each of the three roles.

The tutor will conclude his briefing by saying that he realises that the person in the counselling role is unlikely to complete the counselling in 15 minutes, but that this is long enough for the purposes of training and will provide plenty of information for discussion and learning. He may add that if the interview overruns its time, the observer could give a pre-arranged signal, such as a tap on the chair, so that things can be brought to a conclusion.

Carrying out the counselling exercise

When the three people have assembled in their room, the tutor will briefly check with them to see if they have understood their instructions. He may help them to agree on the batting order and the placing of chairs.

The tutor will usually keep silent, like the observer, during each of the interviews, and make his comments during the evaluation periods. However, he may occasionally have to intervene with a comment during an interview if people are getting out of role or in the unlikely instance that things are going wildly wrong.

During the evaluation period which follows each interview, the tutor has a vital role to play and he must remember his objective, which is to maximise the learning for each member of the trio. One of his main tasks will be to help the observer keep to his proper role of analysing and evaluating the performance of the interviewer. The problems presented are frequently so fascinating and absorbing that the observer is caught up in them and wants to give his own solutions or criticise those that have been discussed. This can result in a very likely discussion, but it is at the expense of the learning. The tutor must gently but firmly point out what is happening and help the observer return to his proper job.

The other task the tutor will have, especially in the first evaluation period, is to raise important points which the observer may have missed. Each evaluation period should include at least the following points:

(a) How did the interview commence?
(b) What kind of relationship was established?
(c) How well were questions used?
(d) Who did most of the talking?
(e) Was the core of the problem revealed?
(f) Were feelings expressed?
(g) Was any advice given?
(h) Did the client feel criticised?
(i) Did the client receive real help?

The effective tutor enhances the exercise not only by contributing to the interview evaluation, but by his own behaviour, because he is in fact acting as counsellor to the group. The performance of each subsequent interview thus clearly improves and the final one is substantially better than the first.

THE FINAL PLENARY DISCUSSION

Following the trios, all the trainees and tutors meet together to discuss their experiences. The tutor should at the start make it clear that this is not the place to discuss the actual problems which were presented in the trios, but rather how they found the actual process of counselling. This again can be a vital stage in the learning process as people try to come to grips with their recent experiences and discover what they must do to improve their own skills.

That each person learns something different is evident from the variety of points that arise at this final session. The hearty, talkative type will learn that it may be better if he can listen rather than speak all the time. The tentative, shy person may grow to realise that with a little more confidence, he can ask direct, pertinent questions that will make him more effective. Others may realise that their manner does not invite confidences and wonder what they can do about it. Yet others may have learnt that they criticise too much and that this antagonises people.

If the day has gone well, all the people attending will have learnt something about themselves and more importantly, about the most valuable skill of helping and counselling a fellow human being.

Appendix II: Further Reading

A. Counselling, consulting and the therapeutic process: some theories, explanations and practical guides.

Axline, V., *Dibs — In Search of Self,* Pelican Books, Harmondsworth, 1973. (A beautifully written true account of the therapy which enabled a boy to find himself)

Clare, A.W. and Thompson, S., *Let's Talk About Me. A Critical Examination of the New Psychotherapies,* BBC, London, 1981.

Dean, H and Dean, M., *Counselling in a Troubled Society,* Quartermaine House, 1981.

Dickson, J.D. and Roethlisberger, F.J., *Counselling in an Organisation,* Harvard University, 1966. (An account of the Hawthorne counselling programme)

Kennedy, E., *On Becoming a Counsellor — A Basic Guide for Non-professional Counsellors,* Gill and Macmillan, 1977.

Kovel, J., *A Complete Guide to Therapy,* Penguin Books, Harmondsworth, 1978.

Lippet G. and Lippet, R., *The Consulting Process in Action,* University Associates, California, La Jolla, 1978.

Patterson, C.H. *Theories of Counselling and Psychotherapy,* Harper & Row (3rd edn.), London 1980.

Rogers, C.R., *Client Centred Therapy,* Constable, 1965.

Schein, E., *Process Consultation,* Addison-Wesley, Reading, Mass., 1969.

Venables, E., *Counselling,* National Marriage Guidance Council 1971, reprinted 1975.

Principles of Counselling, BBC Further Education, London, 1978.

B. Theories and explanations of individual and interpersonal behaviour and development.

Argyle, M., *The Psychology of Interpersonal Behaviour,* Penguin Books, Harmondsworth, 1970.

Bion, W.R., *Experiences in Groups,* Tavistock Publications, London, 1968.

Jung, C.G., *The Undiscovered Self* (trans. by R.F. Hull), Routledge & Kegan Paul, London, 1974.

Rogers, C.R., *On Becoming a Person,* Constable, London, 1961.

Salzberger-Wittenberg, I., *Psycho-Analytic Insight and Relationships — A Kleinian Approach,* Routledge & Kegan Paul, London, 1970.

Storr, A., *The Integrity of the Person,* Pelican Books, Harmondsworth, 1960.

The Seven Ages of Man, New Society Reprint, first published as a series of articles in 1964.

C. Organisational behaviour – Ways in which people behave at work.

Clifton Williams, C., *Human Behaviour in Organisations*, South-Western Publishing Co., 1978.

de Board, R., *The Psychoanalysis of Organisations*, Tavistock Publications, London, 1978.

Handy, C.B., *Understanding Organisations*, Penguin Books, Harmondsworth, 1976.

McGregor, D., *The Human Side of Enterprise*, McGraw-Hill, New York, 1960. (A classic, explaining the famous Theory X and Theory Y)

Schein, E., *Organisational Psychology*, Prentice-Hall, Englewood Cliffs, NJ, 1965.

D. Transactional analysis.

Berne, E., *Games People Play*, Grove Press Inc., 1964; Penguin Books, Harmondsworth. 1968.

Berne, E., *What Do You Say After You Say Hello?*, Bantam Books, 1973.

James, M. and Jongeward, D. *Born to Win*, Addison-Wesley, Reading, Mass., 1971.

Jongeward D. *Everybody Wins: Transactional Analysis Applied to Organisations*, Addison-Wesley, Reading, Mass., 1973.

Klein, M., *Lives People Live*, John Wiley & Sons, New York, 1980.

Wagner, A. *The Transactional Manager*, Prentice-Hall, Englewood Cliffs, NJ, 1981.

E. Understanding health and stress.

Gillie, O. and Mercer, D., *The Sunday Times Book of Body Maintenance*, Michael Joseph, London, 1978.

Melhuish, A., *Executive Health,* Business Books, London, 1978.

Open University, *The Good Health Guide,* Harper & Row, London, 1980.

The BMA Book of Executive Health, Times Books, London, 1979.

Index

135

The David Solution
How to Liberate your Organization
through Empowerment

Valerie Stewart

As Jean Jacques Rousseau neglected to say: 'Organizations were created free, but everywhere they are in chains.' Whether you work in the private or public sector, in service, retailing, manufacturing or utilities, Valerie Stewart's new book will help you to demolish the blockages that prevent people in your organization from consistently delivering peak performance.

Written in a direct and entertaining style and enlivened with anecdotes, parables and case studies, it will show you: how to bust the bureaucracy; how to avoid paralysis by analysis; how to break down the barriers of organizational empire; how to empower junior managers; how to put customers first (yes, truly); and how to create an enabling culture.

Contents

1990   176 pages   0 566 02843 3 Hardback   0 566 07420 6 Paperback

Gower

Face to Face Skills

Second Edition

Peter Honey

Effective people skills are an important aspect of management style. Most managers spend a large part of their time in face to face encounters, whether at formal occasions such as meetings and presentations or in less formal interactions involving two people or more.

In this book, Peter Honey explains that in these situations behaviour patterns – which are not necessarily the most appropriate or effective – are repeated, simply because they 'come naturally'.

Using examples and case studies based on familiar situations he shows how to make behaviour – both spoken and non verbal – a conscious process that can be harnessed and used to help ourselves and the people with whom we work.

Face to Face Skills makes a powerful contribution to improving personal effectiveness and is essential reading for anyone intent on becoming a more effective manager.

Contents

Introducing behaviour • Situations, objectives and behaviour • Exercises in behaviour recognition • Developing realistic objectives • How to analyse behaviour • Exercises in behaviour analysis • How to shape other people's behaviour • Non-verbal behaviour • How to plan behaviour • What is interactive competence?

1990   208 pages   0 566 02873 5

Gower

Gower Handbook of Management
Third Edition
Edited by Dennis Lock

The Gower Handbook of Management first appeared in 1983. It was acclaimed by reviewers and quickly established itself as a standard work. It covers the entire spectrum of management activity: strategy, operations and personal skills.

This third edition follows the pattern on which the success of the earlier editions was based. Its objectives and structure remain the same but the scope has been extended considerably. The text has been thoroughly revised and ten completely new chapters have been added, including chapters on quality and culture. Every chapter now ends with details of further reading for those who wish to pursue any subject in greater depth.

The handbook now contains seventy three chapters, each contributed by an authority on the subject in question. It remains the most comprehensive single-volume guide to management practice in the English language.

Summary of Contents

Part 1: Principles, policy and organization • Part 2: Financial management • Part 3: Marketing and sales management • Part 4: Research, development and design • Part 5: Purchasing and inventory management • Part 6: Production and project management • Part 7: Logistics management • Part 8: Administration • Part 9: Human resource management • Part 10: The skills of management • Index.

1993   1044 pages   Paperback   0 566 07477 X

Gower

The Skills of Leadership

John Adair

Leadership is an essential ingredient in successful management and every manager therefore needs to acquire or develop the skills of leadership. The aim of this book is to provide guidance to that end.

Skills cannot of course be learned from a book alone, and constant practice is vital. What the book does offer is an explanation of the concepts underlying the skills of leadership, supported by a wealth of practical hints, and enlivened by examples drawn from a wide variety of circumstances. The present text has been developed largely by condensing and combining the ideals contained in three of the author's earlier works, with new material added where appropriate. The result is a modern treatment of leadership, decision-making and communication which no manager with 'people problems' can afford to ignore.

Contents

1984   298 pages   0 7045 0555 X

Gower

The Unblocked Manager

A Practical Guide to Self-Development

Mike Woodcock and Dave Francis

This highly practical book is for managers and supervisors who wish to improve their personal effectiveness. In the course of their management development work with hundreds of managers the authors have identified eleven possible 'blockages' on the path to managerial competence. The book explains what these blockages are and how to overcome them. Designed as a self-development package, *The Unblocked Manager* is dedicated to helping managers to make the most of their potential.

Contents

1986   252 pages   0 7045 0523 1

Gower

Becoming the Best
How to Gain Company-wide Commitment to Total Quality

Barry Popplewell and Alan Wildsmith

How could it happen in a buoyant market? New products, lots of orders, and yet no profit – a big fat ZERO. The opportunity had been there – and he'd blown it. As the story unfolds Neil begins to understand the problem.

Quality is the key – not just product quality but total quality. "If everybody was the best at what they do," he thought " then this would be one hell of a company." So that's what he sets out to do – become the best. How he conceives his idea, translates it into practice, cajoles and carries his employees with him, is all in this fascinating book.

Contents

"The day had started bad. It couldn't get any worse." • "Facts...the bright stepping stones of logic." • "No problem's too big. What it needs is a big solution, and the will to do it." • "What it means is, you're not in control." • "One common aim for everybody." • "The organization was rife with rumour." • "He didn't want a navigation officer, he wanted a bomb-disposal squad." • "Improve the whole organization, everybody, everywhere. Impossible?" • "This whole organization is going to be turned upside down." • "Everybody is a supplier and a customer." • "Enthusiasm, a sense of purpose, you don't generate those by pushing a piece of paper under somebody's nose." • "Basic questions like 'Do you know who your customers are?'" • "No more red-label orders, no panics. What a sweet life." • "Best in the world applies to people, not things." • "Hold on to your vision. Stay with it". Epilogue.

1988   156 pages   0 566 02798 4 Hardback   0 566 02877 8 Paperback

Gower